Breakfast Santa Fe Style

A Dining Guide to Fancy,
Funky, and Family Friendly
Restaurants

Breakfast Santa Fe Style

A Dining Guide to Fancy, Funky, and Family Friendly Restaurants

Kathy Barco & Valerie Nye

SUNSTONE
PRESS
SANTA FE

Photography by the authors

Front cover photo: La Fonda Hotel interior by Mike Jaynes

Book Design and Illustration by Mike Jaynes

Sunstone books may be purchased for educational, business, or sales promotional use. For information please write: Special Markets Department, Sunstone Press, P.O. Box 2321, Santa Fe, New Mexico 87504-2321.

Library of Congress Cataloging-in-Publication Data

Barco, Kathy, 1946-

Breakfast Santa Fe style : a dining guide to fancy, funky, and family friendly restaurants / Kathy Barco and Valerie Nye.

p. cm.

ISBN 0-86534-501-5 (softcover : alk. paper)

1. Restaurants--New Mexico--Santa Fe--Guidebooks. 2. Breakfasts--New Mexico--Santa Fe. I. Nye, Valerie, 1971- II. Title.

TX945.B375 2006
647.95789'56--dc22

2005030485

Published in

www.sunstonepress.com

SUNSTONE PRESS / Post Office Box 2321 / Santa Fe, NM 87504-2321 /USA
(505) 988-4418 / orders only (800) 243-5644 / FAX (505) 988-1025

Dedication

This book is dedicated to our parents.

Kyle and Betty Nye – V. N.

Jim and Mildred Falconer – K. B.

Acknowledgements

For visiting restaurants with us, trying new dishes, even sharing "just one bite" . . . for providing editing, proofreading, and marketing help . . . for giving us inspiration, motivation, encouragement, and love . . . the authors wish to thank the following people: Joel Yelich, Robert Upton, Mary Lou Sullenberger, Jim Smith, Relf Price, Kristen Kida, Mike Jaynes, George and Aileen Jaynes, Robin Harris, Don Harris, Beth Harper, Brian Graney, Miriam Bobkoff, LeRoy Barco, and Jeanne-Marie Bakehouse.

Contents

Fancy, Funky, Family Friendly, Fast

Introduction

Breakfast in New Mexico can easily be the most memorable meal of the day. Whether you're here for the first time, a returning visitor, or a longtime resident of Santa Fe, the City Different, we hope you'll savor this book. This is a comprehensive look at most of the restaurants that serve breakfast in Santa Fe. We've tried to include a wide variety of dining options, from quickie burrito stands to fancy weekend brunches, and lots in between.

There are many exciting breakfast options in New Mexico. Traditional foods include tortillas, beans, eggs, chorizo (red sausage), and red and green chile. These tasty elements serve as a palette for the state's artistic cooks and chefs. They mix and match ingredients to create a wide variety of breakfast dishes from the standard breakfast burrito and Mexican omelet to the less traditional blue corn piñon nut French toast and grilled chocolate sandwich.

From the Authors:

We grew up in New Mexico, left the state for college and careers, and are lucky enough to have returned to New Mexico, the Land of Enchantment. Both of us are librarians. In honor of our profession, we have included recommended reading with each restaurant description. We hope each recommended book will add to your enjoyment of local food, places, and culture.

While putting our research skills to work for this comprehensive breakfast guide, we paid for every meal and did not accept donations or comments from restaurant owners or staff (aside from remarks on the hotness of the chile!).

Some Things to Keep in Mind:

Although several of the restaurants have web sites, we've learned not to count on the accuracy of the information posted there, especially concerning menu items and hours of operation. Please be aware that restaurants change menus, hours, prices, décor, and even location. If you are depending on a breakfast location for

your first meal of the day, our advice is to call ahead to verify pertinent information.

We've included a price guide with each description:

$ Average cost for entrée less than $6

$$ Average cost for entrée $6-$10

$$$ Average cost for entrée $11 and up

Although booster and high chairs are available just about everywhere, some restaurants are more prepared than others for the "kid component." Below is the key to our rating system:

* Children welcome, but not an easy restaurant for children and all of their needs.

** The restaurant can easily accommodate one or more children at a table.

*** Children have their own menu and the restaurant can easily accommodate one or more children at a table.

Regarding our restaurant visits, we usually went solo or just the two of us. Sometimes, we included assorted friends and/or spouses. While dining in a group was fun, we discovered that eating alone made it easier to document our experiences.

It's also important to note that we describe the restaurants at fixed points in time. In other words, our visits were a series of snapshots. You might see a different picture when you go.

Many places serve alcohol at breakfast. In accordance with New Mexico state law, on Sundays you will have to wait until noon to enjoy your favorite breakfast alcoholic beverages.

Be prepared for New Mexico's official state question: "red or green?" It refers to which type of chile you would like to have with your meal. If you're not sure, you can ask for both and specify "on the side," that way you can taste for yourself and determine your preference. Most places tend to serve your meal "smothered" in whatever sauce you choose. You can avoid some potential dining

disasters by being picky at first. You won't offend the server by asking for chile on the side.

Above all, enjoy sampling the saucy, subtle, spicy, sweet, succulent flavors of breakfast–Santa Fe Style!

Your taste bud tour guides,

Valerie and Kathy

www.breakfastsantafestyle.com

Adelita's Mexican Restaurant

3297 Cerrillos Road
(505) 474-4897

Breakfast Hours:
Daily 8am-11am
Kid Component: ***
Parking: Plentiful
Area: Cerrillos
Prices: $

You've no doubt heard of bibliotherapy (emotional healing through books). How about eatery-therapy? Let us prescribe Adelita's if you're feeling a little blue, if it's a Monday morning, or if you have the urge to experience really exciting furniture.

Come early, so you'll be able to choose your favorite seating arrangements. Twelve booths and five tables are beautifully embellished with incredible carvings. Do you like exotic birds? Fruit? Jungle animals? The sun and moon? Cactus? How about a dive under the sea with an octopus, a seahorse, and a starfish? Or a siesta by a saguaro? More stimulating is the booth with the carved mountainscape complete with a volcano. One morning when we arrived at Adelita's, the volcano booth was occupied by a family who had evidently recently visited the Valles Caldera in the nearby Jemez Mountains, and the youngsters were still excited about that experience. Since we had been to the Georgia O'Keeffe museum just days before, we were delighted to sit in the calla lily booth.

Adelita's is alive with fantastic and colorful artwork, and even the tabletops get in on the act. It seems a shame to cover these masterpieces with dishes and silverware, but luckily plenty of highlights remain visible under the thick acrylic coating that assures a level eating surface.

Carved sunflowers are everywhere—overhanging the windows, holding the napkins—and flower-filled terra cotta pots hang from the ceiling.

But you're here to eat, right? Many of the breakfast entrées on the

menu feature huevos (eggs). Most of them also include refried beans, potatoes, and tortillas: chilaquiles con huevos (cheese enchilada casserole with red or green chile); chuleta con huevos (10 oz. beef tenderloin); huevos a la Mexicana (eggs mixed with jalapeños, tomatoes, and onions); huevos Adelita's (choice of ham, chorizo, or bacon); huevos ahogados (chip strips); huevos con machaca (shredded beef); huevos con rajas (eggs mixed with green onions and chili ancho); not to mention huevos rancheros, available at the special price of $3.99 weekdays only. If you prefer eggs as a sweet, try the flan (egg custard with caramel sauce) found on the menu under postres (desserts). Cereal, French toast, oatmeal, and pancakes are also available.

Besides the usual beverages, you might choose to try hot chocolate abuelita (like grandma used to make?!), agua de orchata (rice water) or Jarritos (Mexican soda pop). There's a nice array of domestic and imported beers as well, many of them cooling down in the big ice-filled tub resembling a can of Tecate near the front entrance. (And you thought it was just part of the exciting furniture!)

This is a fun place to bring children. Their imaginations will be stimulated by the exotic surroundings. The restaurant has a kids menu, plus plenty of high chairs and booster seats. Be sure to take the youngsters to look at the gigantic carved prickly pear cactus that surrounds the huge carved "Adelita's Restaurant" sign on the back wall. But watch out for the thorns . . . avoid sticky fingers at all costs!

Recommended reading: Speaking of grandmothers, Magda learns a valuable lesson about life and making tortillas from her abuelita in Magda's Tortillas/Las tortillas de Magda *by Becky Chavarría-Cháirez. Discover the fascinating background to the creation of the Valles Caldera National Preserve in* Valle Grande: a History of the Baca Location No. 1 *by Los Alamos resident Craig Martin.*

Atomic Grill

103 East Water Street
(505) 820-2866

Breakfast Hours:
Monday-Thursday 11am-3am,
Friday-Saturday 9am-3am, Sunday
9am-midnight
Kid Component: *
Parking: Street and municipal lots
Area: Plaza
Prices: $$

You won't need security clearance or even a Geiger counter to visit the popular Atomic Grill.

If the season is right, you may be tempted to take a table in the pleasant, shaded outdoor area. Once settled, it's easy to imagine yourself at the nucleus of an atom, surrounded by the sparkling tiny white lights adorning the covered eating area and entwining the patio columns.

Should you choose to sit outside, don't leave without peeking into the restaurant itself. Inside, what might be mistaken for a small atomic reactor is actually a pizza oven. Covered with a predominantly blue mosaic of glass and tile and featuring stars, spirals, and the classic atom design, the pizza oven serves double duty as kitchen equipment and a work of art. The piece gives a kaleidoscope-like view of the night sky, especially when some of the iridescent glass reflects the patio's maze of mini-lights.

While inside, glance at the delectable pastries and desserts in the display case, and marvel at the incredible array of labels on the beer bottles in the cooler. Over 100 different varieties are offered. Free wireless Internet is available inside, at the counter only.

But our subject is breakfast, which is served all day. You should be prepared to experience an atomic reaction of your own (such as "wow!") when your server delivers a plate of raspberry-infused French toast made from fresh challah bread (baked on the premises) and served with apricot butter and warm syrup. There's a definite risk

of "fallout" due to the profusion of sliced fresh strawberries topping the toast triangles.

For a healthful shot of "atomic" energy, try the low-fat oven-baked granola with grain, oats, almonds, brown sugar, cinnamon, raisins, dried cranberries, and dried apricots.

Assemble a custom omelet from an enticing list of potential ingredients, guaranteeing a high satisfaction yield. A tasty payload is delivered in the breakfast burrito, which contains scrambled eggs, fresh homemade hash browns, black beans, and cheddar jack smothered with veggie red or veggie green.

Before you exit, take note of the glowing Atomic Grill sign on the back wall. (Relax, it only glows because it's neon!) On the way out, look up at the small glass windows near the ceiling. The etched panels feature a variety of designs, but the dragonfly is particularly striking.

Recommended reading: Santa Fe is only 34 miles from the real "Atomic City." Find out what a blast it was to grow up there by reading Secrets! of a Los Alamos Kid, 1946-1953 *by Kristin Embry Litchman.*

Aztec Café

317 Aztec Street
(505) 820-0025

Breakfast Hours:
Monday-Saturday 7am-7pm,
Sunday 8am-6pm
Kid Component: **
Parking: Limited parking behind the
restaurant; street and municipal lots
Area: Plaza
Prices: $

Santa Fe, the City Different, has had a long-standing reputation of being a city of free thinkers: artists, writers, people who march to a different drum, and people who don't march at all. Walking around and driving in Santa Fe today, you may wonder if these individualists still live here. Where is Santa Fe's funky element? In the last 20 years or more, the city has catered to tourists and to people with enormous incomes who buy houses in Santa Fe to complement the other vacation homes they own in Nantucket or Paris. As a tourist on a short visit to Santa Fe, it may be difficult to scratch the surface and find the people that put "different" in the city's nickname. However, for those of you on a quest for Santa Fe's counterculture (or just a good time), you should plan to spend a morning at the Aztec Café.

The Aztec Café is a coffee shop with three main breakfast entrées: breakfast burritos, pastries, and bagels. Breakfast burritos are served until noon. Everything else is available all day. Breakfast burritos can be eaten at the café or taken on the run. The burritos come wrapped in foil and include eggs, cheese, black beans, potatoes, and green chile. The restaurant offers a wide selection of bagel options. The Aztec bagel, featuring hummus, avocado, and green chile strips, is sublime! We also really enjoyed the café's great coffee, a rich house blend.

In order to fully appreciate the Aztec Café and its neighborhood, have a seat in one of the two rooms inside the restaurant. The place feels like a Santa Fe home with plaster walls, a fireplace, a couch, tiled tables, and tall barstool chairs. Local art decorates the walls. We were especially taken with the wooden owl and wooden devil hanging

above the order counter. The Aztec has one computer with Internet access available for customers. A nearby sign admonishes, "Please refrain from pouring drinks on the keyboard."

If the weather is nice, venture out, with coffee in hand, onto the crowded side patio and strike up a conversation with any one of the hanger-outers. While enjoying the outdoor conversation, you might encounter a helmeted and sword-carrying five-year old boy with his co-conspiring dog. You might see a long-haired, long-skirted woman pushing a stroller across the street with a German Shepard in tow. You might watch a Golden Retriever walk up and down the restaurant's driveway, and then, out of the corner of your eye, see the dog dash into the restaurant.

Yes, dogs are welcome visitors at the Aztec Café. Water dishes sit outside the restaurant doors, waiting for parched lapping tongues. A jar of dog biscuits sits on the order counter inside the café; treats for our four-footed furry friends.

Recommended reading: Animal lovers will adore the Aztec Café in combination with the book titled People I Sleep With *by Santa Fe artist Jill Fineberg. The book is filled with photographs of people sleeping peacefully with their pets: their dogs, cats, horses, snakes, and scorpions.*

Bagelmania

420 Catron
(505) 982-8900

Breakfast Hours:
Daily 7am-3pm
Kid Component: **
Parking: Plentiful
Area: Midtown
Prices: $$

If Bagelmania were a book, it would have the following subtitle: "A New York Café, Deli, and Bakery." As it says on the menu: "Our goal is to be the best in town." They come pretty close, too!

As librarians, we appreciated this literary allusion on the menu: Goldilox (two scrambled eggs with smoked salmon, cream cheese, and chives, served with potato pancakes and bagel). Other specialties include eggs Yucatecos (two eggs and black beans on a corn tortilla with chili and cheese, served with fried bananas); Lonestar breakfast (tender chicken fried steak, two eggs, creamed gravy); and there's a breakfast burrito as well!

In the "Every Day Brunch Specials" you will find five distinct Benedicts, which include the requisite poached eggs and hollandaise sauce plus: Chesapeake Bay (featuring two blue crab croquettes); Blackstone (tomatoes and avocado); Tex (tomatoes, sausage, and green chile); deluxe (bacon and mushrooms); and Mex (chorizo, tomatoes, green and red chili sauce). There is a variety of omelets, a portabella frittata, blue corn quesadillas, and several huevos dishes including rancheros, rancheros muchos, and divorciados.

You say none of the above has whetted your appetite? How about a short or full stack of the special pancake of the day? Do you happen to be a fan of the Three Stooges? Crack up over the egg dishes named for Moe, Larry, and Curly. By the way, there is a terrific variety of bagels and spreads, too, hence the name, Bagelmania.

Depending on the season, you can sit outside on the deck at one of ten tables shaded by huge umbrellas. The day we sat outdoors, several

musicians from the Santa Fe Opera were seated around a double table. Their cased instruments, three violins and a cello, occupied a nearby table. While waiting for our meals, we quietly speculated about what kind of food the instruments might have ordered. We decided on an omelet made with string cheese, salami, and chile Verdi.

Inside, the floor's black and white linoleum tiles are laid in squares of four, reminding us of a giant chessboard. There are seven stools at the counter, and lots of tables with faux marble tops. The b & w theme continues in the large framed photographs on the wall.

Black and white glossies of Sophia Loren and Clark Gable on the restroom doors are hints about which is which.

All bakery items are made on the premises. On the way out, consider purchasing one of Bagelmania's yummy cookies. Here's your chance to try New Mexico's official state cookie: the biscochito!

Recommended reading: Biscochitos are mentioned in Helen Foster James' children's book E is for Enchantment: A New Mexico Alphabet, *illustrated by New Mexico resident Neecy Twinem. But don't look under "B"—these spicy cookies are listed under "F"—for Favorite Foods!*

Baja Tacos

2621 Cerrillos Road
(505) 471-8762

Breakfast Hours:
Monday-Thursday 7am-9pm,
Friday-Saturday 7am-10pm,
Sunday 8am-9pm
Kid Component: **
Parking: Plentiful
Area: Cerrillos
Price: $

At Baja Tacos, you'll experience a combo plate of history and geography before you even step out of your car. The tri-cultural flavor of New Mexico is depicted on an enormous mural on the north side of the building. Colorful full-length portraits feature Maria Martinez, the famous San Ildefonso potter; Flamenco dancer Maria Benitez; and artist Georgia O'Keeffe. Across the parking lot from the mural is the U-Haul rental headquarters. Depending on what equipment is in, you'll get a geography lesson based on the geo-graphics decorating the trucks and trailers.

In New Mexico, the official state question is "red or green?" But an unofficial question concerns the correct spelling of that pillow-like deep-fried bread: is it "sopapilla" or "sopaipilla?" Luckily, you don't have to know how to spell this delicacy to enjoy it. If you've fallen in love with sopapillas, but thought that they could only be enjoyed with lunch or dinner, think again! At Baja Tacos, you can order this airy New Mexican treat for breakfast.

Actually, you can get anything on their extensive menu: breakfast, lunch, dinner, veggie, house specialties . . . whenever you wish, because everything is served from opening to closing all day. If you think sopapillas are super and have dreamed of eating them for your first meal of the day, wake up to reality at Baja Tacos.

Baja Tacos' veggie menu includes this statement: "We take great care to ensure that our vegetarian items are true to their name. No meat broth is used in our chile stews or salsas and no lard in our fresh pinto beans, tortillas or sopapilla dough!" Consider the stuffed

sopapillas from their veggie menu: fresh sopapilla stuffed with beans or tofu, shredded cheese, vegetarian red or green chile stew, lettuce, tomatoes, and onions.

This "breakfast served all day" concept means you can savor the Baja breakfast combo plate (your favorite breakfast burrito smothered in red or green chile stew, a side of beans, hash browns, and a delicious pork tamale) until 9:00 p.m. most nights, and even later on Friday and Saturday. Conversely, if instead of oatmeal you'd prefer that delectable mélange known as "Frito Pie" say ¡Hola! to Baja.

Don't look for fancy ambience or cute décor at Baja Tacos—here it's all about the food. The drive-through window handles most of the business, but customers can also walk in and place orders at the small counter. A covered enclosure in front of the building provides the only seating and sparse shelter, but it affords an unobstructed view of busy Cerrillos Road.

Recommended reading: The title character's eyes get "as big as sopapillas" in Alice Nizzy Nazzy, the Witch of Santa Fe *by Tony Johnston (illustrated by Tomie dePaola). Having given a southwestern makeover to a classic Russian folktale, Ms. Johnston easily could have called her book:* Baba Yaga, Santa Fe Style.

Bishop's Lodge – Las Fuentes

Bishop's Lodge Road
(505) 819-4035 (800) 732-2240

www.bishopslodge.com

Breakfast Hours:
Daily 7am–10am, Sunday Brunch
Buffet 10:30am-noon
Kid Component: ***
Parking: Plentiful
Area: About 4 miles north of the
Plaza (head north on Washington
Avenue, which turns into Bishop's

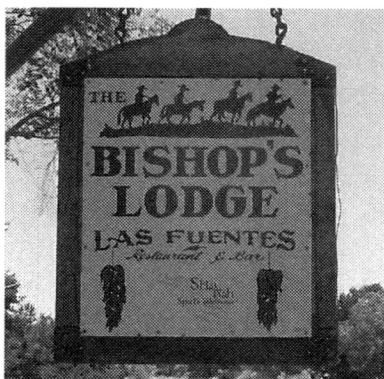

Lodge Road, and watch for the signs
for the turnoff on the right)
Prices: $$$

Breakfast on the outdoor patio of Las Fuentes (the fountains) restaurant at Bishop's Lodge is a captivating experience. Come prepared to spend time enjoying the incredible views, the profusion of blooming flowers, the wonderful sound of the wind in the trees, and a chorus of bird voices.

Don't be surprised if a hummingbird buzzes your table before he dips into the colorful floral buffet that borders the patio. Pansies, petunias, and geraniums aren't on your menu, though. Instead, you'll find delicacies such as blueberry and piñon pancakes garnished with Frangelico Chantilly cream and fresh raspberries, accompanied by butter balls and warm syrup. Or perhaps you'd like to try the buffalo sausage, very tasty and non-greasy. If the hummingbird's method is more your style, the breakfast buffet in the dining room is varied enough to satisfy any taste. Choose from made-to-order omelets, blintzes, pancakes, meats, cereal, fruit, and more. Be sure to sample the fabulous cheesy potatoes that also contain heavy cream, bacon, and chives.

It's hard to believe that others dining in this glorious setting can become engrossed in the *New York Times* instead of basking in the peace and tranquility. By doing this, they miss the nearby ravens, who seem to be cawing "Look around!" The tall cottonwood trees dense with green occasionally release a bright gold leaf that flutters gently to the ground. Is it reminding us to come back when the season

changes? In the fall we could admire the brilliant red of the Virginia creeper, creeping up the back of the outdoor fireplace.

Weekday breakfast starts early enough to accommodate a solo before-work outing, but it would be a great early morning adventure for office-mates as well. The more elaborate Sunday brunch is a really big deal that lends itself to celebrations and entertaining special guests.

Recommended reading: If you've read Willa Cather's masterpiece, Death Comes for the Archbishop, *you'll want to visit the chapel after finishing your meal. (If you haven't read the book yet, it's for sale in the gift shop.) Although the book is a work of fiction, it's closely based on the life of Bishop Jean Baptiste Lamy, who became the Archbishop of Santa Fe in 1875. Lamy bought land in the Tesuque valley, and built a small, private chapel and living quarters as a retreat. Following his death, and several subsequent changes in ownership, the property developed into The Bishop's Lodge Resort. The anteroom of the tiny chapel includes several photos of Lamy, and one of Willa Cather taken in 1927, the year that* Death Comes for the Archbishop *was published. There are also two framed examples of beautiful calligraphy. One gives a brief biographical description of Bishop Lamy. The other contains the passage from chapter nine of the book that details "Father Latour's" retirement to his country estate four miles north of Santa Fe. Included are references to various fruit trees, in particular a giant apricot tree with two trunks. The stump of this tree is still standing today. Visiting Bishop's Lodge and reading the portions of Cather's work that so movingly evoke a "sense of place" combine to provide a powerful eating/literary experience.*

Blake's Lotaburger

Locations serving breakfast:
3200 Cerrillos Road (505) 471-2433
420 Airport Road (505) 473-7633
2820 W. Zia Road (505) 438-2411
404 N. Guadalupe (505) 983-4915

www.lotaburger.com

Breakfast Hours:
Monday–Saturday 7am-10:30am
Kid Component: **
Parking: Ample
Prices: $

"If you are what you eat, you are awesome!" Or at least that's what they'd have you believe at Blake's Lotaburger, a New Mexico tradition for over 50 years. Not quite as ubiquitous as McDonald's, but found only inside New Mexico state lines, Blake's boasts more than 70 locations statewide. Five of these are in Santa Fe, and currently four of the Santa Fe restaurants are in breakfast mode.

Paraphrasing Blake's slogan, "If burritos are what you eat, ours are awesome!" You'll have a choice of six different breakfast burritos, mixing and matching with eggs, cheese, bacon, sausage, hash browns, beans, and red or green chile. These hefty bundles are the "hand held" type, tightly wrapped and easily eaten in the car or on the go, thanks to the fact that they're made "chili in." Knife and fork are definitely called for if you care to add "chili over" (red or green with lettuce, tomato, and cheese).

For variety, try the "Lota Breakfast Sandwich," (Lota toast, eggs, cheese, bacon, and green chile). Add the "chili over" option, and you've got a BLT—Santa Fe style!

Place your order at the counter and then wait for your number to be called. At the Zia, Cerrillos, and Airport locations, you can eat at one of the booths in the spacious dining area. The latter also features a garden-like outdoor patio where you can enjoy your meal in the shade of several red and white striped umbrellas, reminiscent of a forest of giant mushrooms. The Blake's Lotaburger on North Guadalupe has

walk-up ordering, but no indoor seating. There are several outdoor tables underneath a long carport-type covering.

Most New Mexicans have been going to Blake's since childhood, for their distinctive large-diameter Lota Burgers and more diminutive Itsa Burgers. The first location opened in Albuquerque in 1952. For as long as both of us can remember, orders have been written down in pencil on the back of the white paper bag that will eventually hold your food. Most everyone recognizes these distinctive bags with red and blue printing that feature the familiar Lotaburger man. They even appeared on the silver screen (accompanied by much cheering from local audiences) in the 1992 movie "White Sands" starring Micky Rourke, Willem Dafoe, and Sam Jackson (before he became Samuel L.).

Recommended reading: You can't make burritos without tortillas. Find out what else can be done with tortillas in The Tortilla Cat *by Nancy Willard.*

Bumble Bee's Baja Grill

301 Jefferson (505) 820-2862
3777 Cerrillos Road (505) 988-3278

Breakfast Hours:
Monday-Friday 7:30-11:00am,
Saturday-Sunday 11:00am-1:00 pm

www.bumblebeesbajagrill.com

Kid Component: **
Parking: Ample
Prices: $

"B" is all you can be for breakfast at Bumble Bee's, where breakfast burritos bring bundles of buzz. Basically, you'll start with a "humongous" flour tortilla that's filled with cheese and eggs. Then you have plenty of choices to make. First, do you prefer breakfast potatoes or beans? Next, will it be red or green chile, pico de gallo, or Bumble Bee's signature smokey roasted tomato salsa? Decisions, decisions! Further enhancements of bacon, chicken, or steak can be included for an extra charge. Up to this point, you're still in the realm of a "handheld" meal. However, you may opt to have your burrito smothered with red or green chile. That's when you'll need a knife and fork. The basic kid's burrito contains rice, beans, and jack and cheddar cheese.

You can phone in your order, drive up to the restaurant, and staff will bring your food out to you. With locations at either end of town, it's easy to pick up a Bumble Bee burrito.

If you're not in a hurry, by all means eat in. The cheerful décor is just the thing to put you in a great frame of mind for the rest of the day. Bright red and yellow walls feature vibrant paintings and folk art. We've often noticed roosters in breakfast eateries, and Bumble Bee's has a cocky collection too. We've seen papel picado (fancy tissue paper cutout banners) in other restaurants around town. The papel picado hanging from BB's ceiling are made from shiny foil. Crepe paper flowers placed around the restaurant add splashes of color, and piñatas shaped like bumble bees hang from the ceiling, poised

to pay a tableside visit. Biting into a Bumble Bee burrito is as glorious as breaking open a piñata, but with these burritos you don't need a big stick or a blindfold, and you won't be showered with candy and trinkets. Just remember to have a napkin handy!

Besides tables for two or four, you'll find a large community table. Additionally, there is barstool seating at long tables along the windows and overlooking the cooking area. Outdoor seating in the covered patio is available.

It's fascinating to watch the cooks filling orders. Even more interesting is the array of rolls of stickers on a shelf above the prep area. These little fluorescent red circles are applied to the outside wrapper of each item and help keep things straight for the servers and customers inside the restaurant, not to mention the folks coming to pick up their phoned-in orders. Without these important stickers, imagine the confusion in the front seat of the car, as hungry passengers paw through a bag of hot bundles of food not knowing what's what. The labels tell the names of the various dishes, and also help describe the contents (or else they describe what's not in each handmade freshly prepared gem): Rice, Shrimp, Chicken, Lamb, Kids Burrito, Tito Burrito, Bumblebee, Pinto Beans, Steak, Fish, Tomas, Black Beans, Grande Chick, Burrito Grande, No Salsa, No Egg, No Guac, No Sour Cream, No Onion, No Cheese, and so on. Many of the labels refer to menu items that are only available after 11 am.

On one of our visits, we overheard a family discussing the labels. After making lists of the words, it turned into a math lesson. "Let's see, there are seven rolls of labels in each dispenser, and there are seven dispensers, plus some extra rolls on the shelf . . . how many different labels are there?" One youngster suggested that the family should establish a goal of eating their way through the entire Bumble Bee's menu in order to collect an example of each label. This would involve visiting during non-breakfast hours, but the parents seemed inclined to make the effort to amass the entire set. We consider this an admirable and tasty goal.

Recommended reading: George Ancona is an award-winning photographer and author of books for young readers. He lives in Santa Fe. His bilingual book, The Piñata Maker/El piñatero *won a Parent's Choice Award.*

The Burrito Company

111 Washington Avenue
(505) 982-4453

Breakfast Hours:
Monday-Friday 7:30am-11am,
Saturday-Sunday 8am-11am
Kid Component: **
Parking: Street and municipal lots
Area: Plaza
Prices: $$

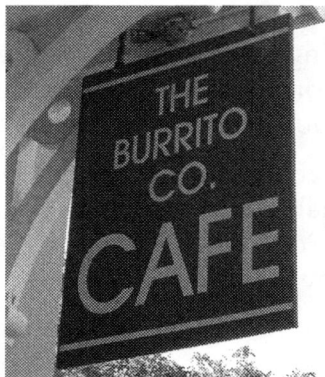

Book lovers in Santa Fe know all about Washington Avenue. The 100 block of Washington Avenue has more books per square foot than any block in Santa Fe. Santa Fe Public Library's main library is located at 145 Washington Avenue, and The Palace of the Governors Fray Angélico Chávez History Library is located at 120 Washington Avenue. Burrito eaters interested in buying books will also be pleased to find the Palace of the Governors Gift Shop right across the street from the Burrito Company on Washington Avenue.

The Burrito Company can be loud and bustling, but for a fast, good, New Mexican breakfast near the Plaza, stop by for a delicious experience. Specials are written on a blackboard outside the restaurant, so be sure to scan for good food ideas before you even open the door. As you come through the doors, grab a menu just inside. Place your order at the counter, and take a seat inside or outside while you wait for your number to be called (the restaurant has a loudspeaker outside, so you will hear your number no matter where you sit).

The Burrito Company has a surprisingly extensive menu. There are numerous low carb options including low carb chile, cheese eggs and low carb chorizo scramble (chorizo and egg topped with sour cream). There is a wide selection of espresso drinks, hot teas, and other hot drinks including hot caramel apple cider.

The Burrito Company wouldn't be a burrito company without burritos. Not surprisingly, you will find a large selection of breakfast burrito options at this restaurant. There are four different handheld burritos available for eating on the run: egg and potato, egg and

bacon, egg and chorizo, and egg with carne adovada. These same four burritos are also available as plates. The plate burritos are smothered in red or green chile and served with a side of potato slices.

We thoroughly enjoyed our breakfast burrito, but the Burrito Company does not stop at making great burritos, they also make some fantastic breakfast plates. During our visit, we happily devoured the papas rancheras (potatoes topped with eggs, cheese, red or green chile all served with a side of sour cream, lettuce, tomato, and tortillas). The eggs were fluffy, and the potatoes were well cooked and a perfect addition to the cheesy eggs.

People in Santa Fe love their dogs, and eating on the patio at the Burrito Company allows for primetime dog watching. Short skinny Daschunds growl at tall white fluffy dogs. Elegantly matured Greyhounds stroll the shaded street walking towards the public library. Excited wooly furred black dogs pull their owners with leash in-hand across the street in their dash toward the awe-inspiring historic Plaza.

Recommended reading: To truly understand the life of a dog, read one of Stephen Huneck's books: My Dog's Brain, Sally Goes to the Beach, *or* Sally Goes to the Mountains. *Huneck's Santa Fe gallery, located at 129 Water Street, is a short walk from the Burrito Company.*

Café Dominic

320 South Guadalupe
(505) 982-4743

Breakfast Hours:
Daily 7:30-3pm
Kid Component: ***
Parking: Street and municipal lots
Area: Plaza
Prices: $$

There is something for everyone at Café Dominic. The restaurant has a whimsical sophistication for adults, and kids are well taken care of with pre-meal activities and comfortable space for erratic dining movement. This is a moderately quiet café, with excellent food options for locals, visitors, adults, and children.

Entering the restaurant you will pick up a bright yellow menu near the front door. Peruse the menu variety. The thick French toast, omelets, fresh cinnamon rolls, or a traditional American breakfast may tempt you. For an "off the egg-beaten path," try tratoria focaccia (fresh basil pesto, sliced tomatoes, and eggs atop a piece of grilled focaccia bread served with dilled potatoes). Children might order a child size buttermilk pancake meal, French toast, or the bull's eye egg (eggs cooked in a cut-out center of a slice of sourdough toast served with bacon or sausage).

Upon placing your order, you will be given a giant order number to place on your table and breakfast will be brought to you. Choose any table in the restaurant. There is one excellent table near the front door, a booth with a window view of Guadalupe Street. Even if you miss this excellent table, there are many great places to sit and admire your surroundings throughout the restaurant. While waiting for breakfast, children will enjoy choosing from a huge variety of coloring pages (look for the file folder box in the restaurant's main room).

A tea party and kitchen art theme adorn the walls and ceilings of the café. Tea cups, coffee cups, and fun dangly mobiles hang everywhere.

Ordinary kitchen utensils hung from ceilings and doorways become objects of intrigue. Tables are topped with buckets filled with silverware and clear jars filled with soda straws.

When breakfast arrives, you won't be disappointed. Breakfast burritos are too big to eat in one sitting and are filled with eggs, caramelized onions, and dilled potatoes. The caramelized onions are a distinctly gourmet touch. Many entrées are served with the dilled potatoes and should not be missed. The potatoes are a surprisingly tasty and comforting breakfast addition. Breakfast burritos come topped with a homemade chile sauce and a side of pinto beans. The meat options in the burrito are wonderful. Our burrito came with thick, sweet, chewy bacon.

The piñon blue corn pancakes also come highly recommended. Pancakes are served on a bright Fiestaware plate with warm syrup on the side. You will find at least one whole piñon nut in each bite of these pancakes . . . a tasty, rich breakfast.

Don't miss the drinks at Café Dominic. The fresh squeezed orange juice is perfect with any meal. The flavored teas are amazing (try the mango and cherry for starters). The café's specialty drink is iced coffee (freshly brewed coffee poured over ice cubes made of coffee), the perfect drink on a warm southwest morning.

While eating at the Café Dominic is a true delight with an attentive wait staff, the café also does a lot of to-go business. Pick up a to-go menu right inside the front door. Whether dining in or eating out, Café Dominic does not disappoint.

Recommended reading: Kids will enjoy the New Mexico-themed coloring book, Santos of Spanish New Mexico *by Al Chapman.*

Café Paris

31 Burro Alley
(505) 986-9162

Breakfast Hours:
Tuesday-Sunday 8am-11:30am;
Summers daily 7am-11:30am

www.cafeparisnm.com

Kid Component: *
Parking: Street and municipal lots
Area: Plaza
Prices: $$

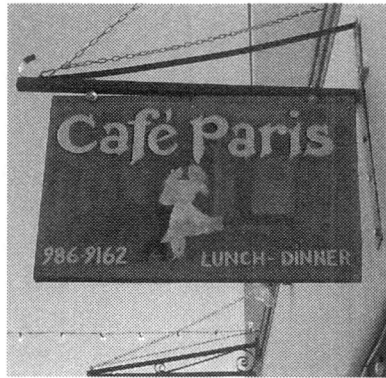

You'll feel like an American in Paris at this charming café, or as it says right over the door, "a true Montmartre bistro." To eat here, you won't need a passport or even a French dictionary! Cleverly hidden in historic Burro Alley, just a *promenade* from the Plaza, a person might not even notice the Café Paris unless the weather happens to be warm enough for the outside tables and umbrellas to be set up in the street. But you don't have to be Hercule Poirot to find this place, once you decide to investigate the source of the enticing aromas wafting out the door.

Don't resist the impulse to walk up to the display of fresh homemade pastries. Brioches, croissants (plain, almond, or chocolate) raisin rolls, palmiers, lemon tarts, raspberry scones, and a bounty of beautiful cookies are artistically arranged. Maybe you'll want to take some of these delights with you when you leave.

Meanwhile, it's time for *le petit-déjeuner*. Two entire pages of the six-page menu are devoted to omelets and eggs. There are eight omelets to chose from, starting with plain and working up through ratatouille (stuffed with eggplant, zucchini, onion, tomatoes, green pepper, and melted Swiss cheese). Although we strive to sample a variety of menu items on our visits, the omelet lyonnaise always ends up in front of one of us. It contains a superb combination of sautéed onion and bacon, and is topped with lusciously melting shredded Swiss cheese. If your taste buds prefer spinach or ham, try the omelet toscane or the omelet au jambon. If you're not exactly *la vie en rose* type, but instead prefer *la vie en chile*, then the chorizo or chipotle omelets are

your style. Lovers of poached eggs are not forgotten at the Café Paris: say *bonjour* to eggs Benedict and Florentine.

Feeling like some dessert to add *joie de vivre* to breakfast? The repertoire includes crème brulée, chocolate mousse, profiterole, apple tatin, tiramisu, café liegeois, mamadou, napoleon, black forest cake, and California tart.

Weather permitting, dine *alfresco*. Outside, over 20 tables are covered with flowery yellow oilcloth. Huge green umbrellas provide shade. Take time to admire the huge mosaic on the wall of the building facing the café. It memorializes the Lensic Theater (now the Lensic Performing Arts Center), a Santa Fe landmark right around the corner on San Francisco Street.

The café's interior affords more than a *soupçon* of French flavor. Murals on the walls and ceilings portray Notre Dame Cathedral, the Eiffel Tower, Montmartre, the Moulin Rouge, and the Seine, plus scenes of the can-can and Parisians being Parisians. *Naturellement*, there are framed Lautrec and Mucha posters. The colorful rooster, which looks right at home hanging near the main entrance, is a print of an original oil done by Santa Fe's acclaimed guitar virtuoso, Antonio Mendoza.

Other touches we love here include the lace curtains and the wire Eiffel Tower on top of the pastry case.

Recommended reading: We bet you're feeling guilty for choosing that profiterole for breakfast, n'est-ce pas? Let us recommend French Women Don't Get Fat: The Secret of Eating For Pleasure *by Mireille Guiliano. Take two chocolate croissants and call us in the morning.*

Café Pasqual's

121 Don Gaspar
(505) 983-9340
(800) 722-7672

www.pasquals.com

Breakfast Hours:
Monday-Saturday 7am-3pm,
Sunday Brunch 8am-2pm

Kid Component: *
Parking: Street and municipal lots
Area: Plaza
Price: $$

Have you ever wondered what it would be like to be in the eye of a hurricane? How about in the eye of a fiesta? Welcome to Hurricane Pasqual—make that Café Pasqual's. Don't worry, you won't be blown away, except maybe by the incredible food, which has been served here for 25 years.

Since the restaurant's official capacity is 49 patrons (according to the sign near the door), be prepared to wait for seating. Should you need some reading material to pass the time, elbow your way to the cash register and purchase a copy of the *Café Pasqual's Cookbook* (subtitled *Spirited Recipes from Santa Fe*). If you arrive early, ask for a table on the upper level near the window. This will give you an excellent view of the wall murals by the renowned Mexican painter Leovigildo Martinez, depicting the moon reveling at her fiesta. Rows and rows of *papel picado*, intricately cut tissue paper banners, flutter above you from the ceiling.

One of our favorite dishes of all time is at this restaurant: Pasqual's version of the breakfast quesadilla. This luscious entrée includes perfectly prepared scrambled eggs, cheese, and the best breakfast guacamole you may ever experience. This is all sandwiched between nicely toasted wheat tortillas, and served with a side of gourmet salsa.

One of our frequent breakfast companions hardly ever wavers from the smoked trout hash (golden hash brown potatoes topped with two poached eggs, and a "scatter" of smoked trout, served with

tomatillo chile d'arbol salsa). However, he has been known to order the huevos motuleños – (Yucatán style eggs over easy on corn tortillas with black beans topped with sautéed bananas, feta cheese, peas, and salsa fresca, served with green chile or tomatillo salsa). Bananas for breakfast? Sounds like just the dish for *Jorge el Curioso*. Jorge would probably also love tamal dulce (sweet corn and raisin tamal wrapped in banana leaves, served with black beans, fresh fruit, and Mexican hot chocolate).

Pasqual's uses only natural and organic ingredients, including organic eggs and naturally raised beef, pork, and lamb. The sausage and chorizo are made on the premises, the chicken is free range and organically raised, and all produce is organic. There's nary a pink, blue, or yellow packet of artificial sweetener in sight. Instead you'll find packs of Xylitol (all-natural wood sugar) or honey.

There are several small tables on both levels, plus one booth. If you happen to be dining alone, or your party doesn't require the intimacy of its own table (and you enjoy serendipitous happenings), join the large "community table." It seats 10, and is ideal for general discussions and the sharing of information among strangers.

A woman across from us at the community table, who had ordered the fried blue and yellow cornmeal mush, asked the server where she could purchase blue cornmeal to take home to New Jersey, and mentioned she was also looking for blue corn hominy. Since we had recently been to the Farmers Market and seen blue hominy for sale at a booth there, we felt comfortable chiming in with this valuable piece of information.

The Sunday brunch menu contains some items not available during the week, including Maga's cheese blintzes, grilled line caught wild salmon burrito and the blue lady enchilada.

Recommended reading: To decorate your own ceiling, Café Pasqual's style, consult Making Magic Windows: Creating Papel Picado/Cut-Paper Art *by Carmen Lomas Garza.*

Café Pink

410 Old Santa Fe Trail
(505) 983-0141

www.thepinkadobe.com/
cafepink.php

Breakfast Hours:
Daily 7am-11am
Kid Component: **
Parking: Street and municipal lots
Area: Plaza
Prices: $$

The Pink Adobe has been a favorite restaurant for many Santa Feans since its establishment in 1944, and it sits amongst some of the city's most historic buildings. The building the restaurant currently occupies is said to be more than 300 years old. The San Miguel Mission, or the "Oldest Church," is right across the street from this historic restaurant.

The Pink Adobe doesn't sell breakfast, but its newborn cousin next door, Café Pink, serves up breakfast in a casual hip coffee shop atmosphere. Almost all breakfast items at the Café Pink are served all day. If, however, you are coming to the café for cereal, you will have to arrive before 11:00 a.m. Oatmeal and cold cereal are only available for early morning breakfasters.

Café Pink offers bagels, scones, empanadas, and muffins. Many of these sweet breakfast items are made at Santa Fe's Chocolate Maven and are packaged for Café Pink. The café also serves an assortment of breakfast burritos. Burritos come with eggs, fried potatoes, corn, bell peppers, and cheese. Other burrito options include the additions of bacon, green chile, and/or vegetables to the standard breakfast burrito model. These burritos are not Santa Fe's typical burritos. They are not smothered in chile, they are not as juicy as you might expect, and they come topped with a slice of jalapeño. You will need a fork and knife to dig into this thick burrito.

Café Pink is becoming widely known in town for its tasty version of New Orleans' favorite pastry, beignets. Beignets are made fresh for

each order. As we sat in the restaurant, men raved, women cried, and children sang about this sweet breakfast treat.

The café boasts a large selection of specialty coffees and teas. Since the Café Pink is also attached to the Dragon Room Bar, this small café is able to offer some wonderful alcoholic specialty drinks including the café margarita, sangria, the rosalita (a cranberry margarita), the pinkie (lemonade with Absolut Citron) and the belini (peach purée and champagne).

The Café Pink has both inside and outside dining with jazz music piped throughout all the areas of the restaurant. Insider diners will experience an elegant café with copper tables topped with cobalt blue bottles filled with fresh flowers. The café rotates its artwork, so there is always a new reason to step into this street side café.

Outside, diners will bask in New Mexico's warm, dry air and watch tourists walk down Old Santa Fe Trail on their way to Santa Fe's Plaza. Whether you choose alfresco dining or not, take a moment to drink in the mural under the Café Pink's portal. It depicts Santa Fe's history and includes images of the Spanish soldiers arriving on horses, St. Francis Cathedral, the Santa Fe Trail, and Santa Fe's oldest church.

Recommended reading: The Pink Adobe has its very own cookbook not surprisingly called, The Pink Adobe Cookbook, *by the restaurant's original 1944 founder, Rosalea Murphy. In Betty E. Bauer's book,* My City Different: A Half-Century in Santa Fe, *she recounts the memories of her many trips to the Pink Adobe.*

Celebrations

613 Canyon Road
(505) 989-8904

Breakfast Hours:
Daily 8am-11am
Kid Component: *
Parking: Free street parking
Area: Plaza
Prices: $$

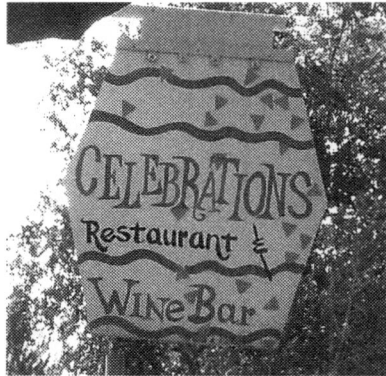

There's a man sitting in the bathroom! At Celebrations, yes, there is! At Celebrations, you will be tickled to find many great surprises at this downtown restaurant.

Celebrations is the only restaurant that serves breakfast on Santa Fe's famed Canyon Road. It is no surprise that artists arriving in Santa Fe in the early 1900s began calling Canyon Road home, with its thick-walled adobe abodes. Today, nearly every square inch of lower Canyon Road is home to a gallery. Most galleries open at 10:00 a.m. when the day comes alive with tourists, artists, gallery owners, and art admirers. An early morning cup of coffee while sitting cradled amongst the warm adobe walls in the quiet hours before the galleries open is the quintessential Santa Fe morning experience.

Indoor and outdoor seating are both delightful at Celebrations. Inside, you are choosing to be seated in the comforts of a traditional thick-walled Canyon Road home. One breakfast room is entirely enclosed and houses small café tables and chairs. Local art hangs on the interior walls, and a mesmerizing round stained glass window flirts with your eye. A kiva fireplace warms the room, even when there isn't a fire blazing. Another restaurant space is neither quite inside nor outside. This patio room has brick floors and adobe walls enclosing three sides. The room is filled with comfortable metal furniture. Sitting outside in front of the restaurant, you can see the famed road and its dog walkers, morning joggers, and an occasional slow driving old pick-up truck.

As the morning moves on, the restaurant begins to fill with business men wearing shorts and t-shirts making real estate deals, a tourist

couple poring through their guide book planning their day of art appreciation, and a group of Spanish speaking intellectuals discussing their upcoming trip to Colombia. With half a cup of coffee in hand, take a deep breath and smell the faint scent of piñon smoke from a distant fireplace.

As if the atmosphere isn't enough, the food is the icing on the cake. Breakfasts include a variety of omelets including the bacon avocado and cheese omelet and the vegetable omelet (red peppers, green peppers, and onions folded into light fluffy eggs). Basic tamales are deliciously dolled up as Mexican corn tamale cakes, with the addition of eggs, corn, peppers, cheese, and chile. Celebrations also has a sweeter side to breakfast with fresh fruit, pancakes, French toast, and heavenly hots (a cute and tasty breakfast with twelve small silver dollar-sized pancakes served with maple syrup). The chef will make small servings for children.

About that man in the bathroom....a papier-mâché man dressed in western attire (sombrero, western jacket, and cowboy boots) sits happily in the bathroom. The day of our visit, he was contentedly holding a jar of flowers and a roll of toilet paper.

Recommended reading: For a peek inside Canyon Road's contemporary art world, pick up a copy of Why I Won't Be Going to Lunch Anymore *by Canyon Road artist Douglas E. Atwill.*

Chocolate Maven

821 West San Mateo Road
(505) 984-1980

www.chocolatemaven.com

Breakfast Hours:
Monday-Friday 7am-10am,
Saturday 8am-11am
Kid Component: *
Parking: Plentiful
Area: Midtown
Prices: $$

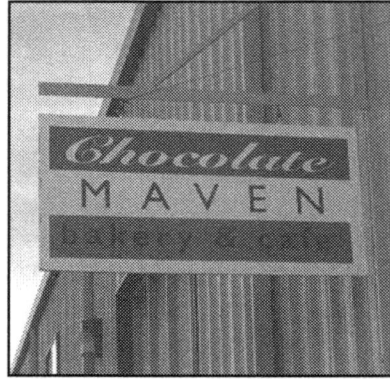

If you are a first-timer to the Chocolate Maven, it may be a little difficult to find, but once you discover this restaurant, you'll be glad you made the effort. It's located in a warehouse building just off San Mateo Road directly behind a Toyota Lexus repair shop. Have your passengers search for a small brown and yellow Chocolate Maven sign. Turn into the Toyota Lexus repair shop parking lot and continue driving down the side of the warehouse. You will find the entrance to the Chocolate Maven mid-building. For more detailed directions, visit the Web site listed above.

While the exterior is a bit austere, just inside the Maven's door you will find the elegant world of a French café. The dining area is two stories of white tableclothed seating surrounded by paintings and dainty lace curtains.

If you are dining alone, you will feel comfortable spending time at this café with a newspaper or the page-turning novel you have been unable to put down. If you are entertaining friends, family, co-workers, or clients, you will find a relaxing atmosphere in which to pass an inspiring hour punctuated with luscious breakfast entrées.

The menu is replete with traditional favorites such as breakfast burritos and a wide variety of omelet options. We would encourage you, however, to step away from the ordinary at the Chocolate Maven and try something new. The breakfasts we ordered were all magnificent, and while we came with a healthy morning appetite, we could not finish our large portions.

Prior to our visit, we had been urged to try the banana walnut buttermilk pancakes, and we weren't disappointed. The small stack featured toasted walnuts and caramelized bananas, and was complemented by a side order of applewood smoked bacon cooked exactly as specified. We also enjoyed the giant serving of peach compote French toast (whipped cream cheese sandwiched between large perfectly grilled pieces of French toast with a compote topping of peach, raisin, and currants). We also recommend the eggsadilla, the Maven's breakfast version of the quesadilla. This entrée is a beautiful presentation of scrambled eggs and cheese gently placed between two tortillas, and topped with black beans, salsa, sour cream, and poblano chiles.

The menu also includes vegetarian dishes such as Santa Fe scrambled tofu. Healthy sides include veggie sausage, veggie bacon, and turkey sausage.

We enjoyed our meal while seated in front of the large picture windows facing the restaurant's industrial bakery. We watched bakers make the day's supply of gigantic cinnamon buns and chocolate filled croissants. These tasty gourmet pastries can be eaten in the elegant dining space or picked up with your cup of coffee on the go. The latter seems like a great option since we had no room to sample any of the Maven's chocolate at breakfast.

Recommended reading: The Chocolate Maven was founded by poet and writer Judyth Hill. The Maven gained a following among Santa Fe writers in the seventies who came for the brownies and community connections. Pláticas: Conversations with Hispano Writers of New Mexico *by Nasario García is a book including interviews with six New Mexico authors: Rudolfo A. Anaya, Denise E. Chavez, Erlinda Gonzales-Berry, E.A. "Tony" Mares, Orlando Romero, and Sabine R. Ulibarri.*

Cloud Cliff Bakery

1805 2nd Street
(505) 983-6254

*www.kanseki.net/cloudcliff/
index.shtml*

Breakfast Hours:
Monday-Friday 7:30am-11am,
Saturday-Sunday 8am-3:30pm
Kid Component: *
Parking: Plentiful
Area: Midtown
Prices: $$

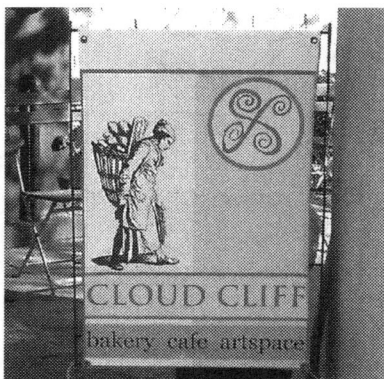

Art and breakfast commingle perfectly at the Cloud Cliff Bakery. Art can be found nearly everywhere in Santa Fe, but you don't need to be on the Plaza or on Canyon Road to enjoy Santa Fe's artists' works. This large loft style restaurant displays local artists' work on long art-loving walls.

Off-street parking is available in an area between the Cloud Cliff and another warehouse. The parking lot is paved with brick, giving a European feel to the bakery before you even enter the restaurant.

Cloud Cliff is located in a giant yellow warehouse. The large dining room has several nice window seats. Café tables are set atop a hardwood floor that was recycled from a local gym. Artwork hangs from the walls, from the ceiling, and above the breakfast/lunch counter. The tables and chairs are wood and metal, both modern and comfortable. Amazing outdoor seating options are available in warmer months.

For breakfast on the run, stop just inside the front door and order an espresso and peruse the bakery case for pastry on the go. Choices range from giant muffins to luscious Danish and beautiful cinnamon rolls.

In order to enjoy the full Cloud Cliff experience, dining-in is highly recommended. The menu is both exotic (in the clouds) and down to earth. High in the sky options include the chilaquiles, which are fried corn tortilla shells filled with avocados, goat cheese, eggs, and green

chile. Truly out of this world. Vegetable pancakes made with spelt and yellow cornmeal served with roasted tomatoes, goat cheese or mozzarella, and topped with sour cream might also send your day high into the atmosphere.

Our down-to-earth favorites include any pastry or bread in the front display with organic coffee and fresh orange juice. The traditional eggs Benedict served on herb ciabatta bread with ham and tomato was a morning delight.

Recommended reading: The main character in Isabel's Daughter *by Judith Ryan Hendricks visits the Cloud Cliff Bakery for a midmorning breakfast.*

Cottonwoods

132 West Water Street
(505) 983-1615

*www.coyotecafe.com/
cottonwoods.htm*

Breakfast Hours:
Seasonal; call for current hours
Kid Component: *
Parking: Street and municipal lots
Area: Plaza
Prices: $$

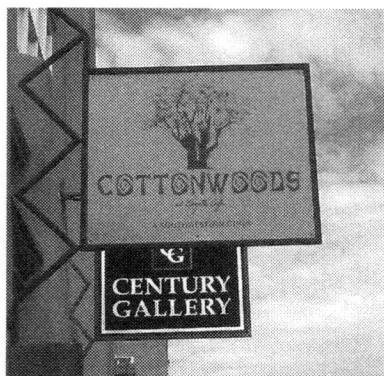

When you first enter Cottonwoods, you might have the urge to play hide and seek. First, the hide: the backs of all the chairs and barstools are covered with hide . . . cowhide. And not from just one breed of cow, either. This is a really varied and colored herd. It's probably a good bet that any cowboy or cowgirl would feel at home on this range. You won't have to lasso these dogies, either. Whoopiee ti yi yo!

Next, the seek: if you're seeking some breakfast choices with definite Santa Fe style, you're on the right trail. And you won't even have time to count to 100 before the menu arrives. Prior to ordering, however, you might want to seek the advice of your server, or even fellow diners. No matter what you finally choose, we're sure you'll be happy with what you find. And later, when you stroll out on the streets of Santa Fe, your hat will be thrown back and your spurs'll be a jinglin'.

Meanwhile, back at the ranch . . . despite the calendar, we went with triple decker Christmas enchiladas (New Mexican-style stacked corn tortillas, layered with scrambled eggs, asadero cheese, refried bandido beans, and Christmas sauce). Nearby diners were raving about the chilaquiles, so we tried them too: chilaquiles con huevos cabrados (extra large scrambled eggs layered with chilaquiles, red chile sauce, and topped with Asadero cheese, guacamole, salsa fresca, sour cream, and fresh herbs). [Note: chilaquiles are tortilla strips combined with other ingredients to soften them up. The dish often resembles a casserole.] Other yummy-sounding offerings include: huevos revueltos con chorizo (three extra large scrambled eggs cooked with

homemade chorizo, served with warm flour tortilla, guacamole, and salsa fresca); omelet a la Mexicana (three egg omelet filled with jack cheese and a choice of chicken tinga, chorizo or grilled vegetables, topped with chipotle and fresh avocado and orange salsa); huevos divorciados; huevos rancheros; the Rio Grande breakfast burrito; and the New Mexican blue corn plate (two blue corn pancakes served with two eggs, fried or scrambled, and bacon).

The television over the bar was showing the Food Channel, but nothing on that screen compared with the food coming from the Cottonwoods kitchen. We were able to observe the chefs cooking in front of an attractive basket-weave patterned brick wall. Every dish we saw, whether placed before us or en route to another table, looked like it was ready for its television close-up.

Speaking of the bar, diners who are so inclined can choose to sip a cocktail in addition to wine and beer. (Not until noon on Sunday, though!)

We were delighted to discover Cottonwoods. It's great to have another moderately priced restaurant so close to the Plaza. The service was excellent, and we overheard this enthusiastic comment: "I like this — cloth napkins!"

Recommended reading: For some mighty enjoyable poems to read by campfire light (or any light), round up a copy of Home on the Range: Cowboy Poetry *selected by Paul B. Janeczko. Bernie Fuchs beautifully illustrated the 19 selections.*

Counter Culture Café

930 Baca St.
(505) 995-1105

Breakfast Hours:
Monday-Friday 8am-11am,
Saturday 8am-3pm,
Sunday 8am-2pm
Parking: Limited space, use dirt lot
across the street
Kid Component: **

Area: Cerrillos
Price: $$

The Counter Culture Café may have been born in opposition to Santa Fe's "high" art and culture, but today it finds itself in the center of Santa Fe's hip and trendy, up and coming Baca neighborhood. Counter Culture is located in a short warehouse building, right next door to a yoga center and down the street from a growing district of Santa Fe's art galleries. Don't get us wrong, Baca Street is a far cry from the atmosphere that attracts so many Santa Fe visitors to Canyon Road, but in the next five to ten years, this sleepy part of town will create its own cultural epicenter.

It may be difficult to find parking at Counter Culture because of the large number of yogis practicing in the area next door, but don't be discouraged, parking is usually less crowded in the dirt lot across the street. Once the car is parked, you will inevitably walk by three or four vehicles with happy dogs anxiously awaiting the return of their peaceful owners.

Stepping in to the restaurant, you will find the menu and ordering station to your left. Drinks and meal options are written in white chalk on blackboards next to and behind the ordering counter. Specialty drinks include espressos, mochas, hot chocolate, and hot and cold teas. Coffees are served in large bowl-like mugs adorned with the Counter Culture Café logo.

The blackboard to the far left of the ordering station announces breakfast options, including smothered and handheld breakfast burritos (beware, we found the green chile quite hot), a three egg omelet with buffalo mozzarella (made from buffalo milk), pesto, and

tomato served with toast and home fries, and an amazing Prosciutto egg sandwich served with fried eggs, red peppers, ham, and Swiss cheese.

Sweet treats include French toast and buttermilk pancakes with an option of fresh blueberries when they are available. The hot muffins are also an outstanding sweet treat. During our visit, warm blackberry muffins were sitting by the register waiting to be snatched up and enjoyed immediately. Other wonderful breakfast options include fresh fruit and hot oatmeal.

When you place your order, you will be handed a number for your table. Before you take a seat, grab the necessary utensils, sauces, salt and pepper, napkins, and straws from the baker's rack just opposite the cash register. When your food is ready, white-aproned cooks will rush around the restaurant looking for your number and will deliver your meal to your table.

Counter Culture's atmosphere is distinctly industrial. Gray cement floors are beneath your feet and metal chairs slide easily under wooden tables with glass tops. Outside seating is available, making this one of the few places where you can eat breakfast inches off of Cerrillos Road while seated beneath large deciduous trees. Outside seating is more desirable if you have come to this café with a friend you intend to talk to over your meal. Inside, the food preparation sounds and talking of restaurant patrons can escalate to a roar in this open space.

Recommended reading: Santa Fe is a town of many remarkable and priceless cultures. Look for Andrew Leo Lovato's Santa Fe Hispanic Culture: Preserving Identity in a Tourist Town.

Cowgirl Hall of Fame BBQ & Western Grill

319 South Guadalupe Street
(505) 982-2565

*www.santafenow.com/rest/cowgirl/
index.html*

Breakfast Hours:
Saturday-Sunday 8:30am-1pm
Kid Component: ***
Parking: Street and municipal lots

Area: Plaza
Prices: $$

If you've always considered yourself a buckaroo or buckarette (or perhaps a *geezer*) at heart, once you enter the Cowgirl Hall of Fame you'll be back in the saddle again, even if you've never actually been in a saddle. This place is really a shrine to the cowgirl, and there's a whole passel of memorabilia to prove it, including a framed photo of Dale Evans.

If you're feeling lucky, it might be due to the profusion of horseshoes used in the décor. You probably spotted the big horseshoe surrounding a cowgirl on the carved sign hanging near the street. Once you enter the patio, glance up to see the traditional double-horseshoes-forming-a-W in "Cowgirl" on the big sign on the front of the building over the main entrance. Once inside, you won't have to look any further than your red and white check-covered table. The salt and pepper, ketchup, and Tabasco are corralled in a holder made of horseshoes that also keeps the little galvanized pails holding sugar and sweetener packets from straying.

The Cowgirl Hall of Fame serves breakfast only on weekends, a good excuse to put on your western duds and hit the trail to Santa Fe. Lucky you . . . the food here is probably a durn sight better than what was served during the roundup or even the rodeo!

Coming out of chute #1: huevos rancheros (two eggs any style cooked to order, stacked atop corn tortillas and black beans, then smothered with your choice of chile and melted jack cheese, and served with flour tortillas and home fries). Cowgirl's home fries are delicious –

just the right amount of onion!

You might need a lasso to hold down your blueberry pancakes. They're so light and fluffy that they fall off the fork. If you're hankering for a burrito, take your pick: breakfast burrito (two farm-fresh eggs cooked the way you like them and served with your choice of grits or home fries with Texas toast) or the vegetarian burrito (scrambled eggs, green chile, potatoes, and jack cheese with grilled tomatoes and asparagus).

Other menu items guaranteed to stick to your ribs include: ranch skillet migas, cowgirl Benedict, ranchers breakfast, biscuits and gravy, and a big bowl o'grits with a sprinkle of cheddar cheese and a pat of butter. The kids' menu includes silver dollar pancakes (a good chance for a little lesson on the history of money!).

The first thing you spot when you come in the door is a huge poster for the Randolph Scott western movie "Santa Fe." Other Cowgirl must-sees: a framed print of "C is for Cowgirl" signed by the artist herself, Spencer Kimball, a Santa Fe resident; "Ginger," the toy horse on wheels; and the framed child-sized chaps, with the name "Sandy" spelled out in barbed wire.

At the end of your meal, you'll see the phrase "Happy Trails" printed on your bill. That sentiment is echoed on the back side of the Cowgirl sign you first saw from the street. It's a cinch that it won't be long 'til we meet again.

Recommended reading: Holding the Reins: A Ride through Cowgirl Life *by Santa Fe author Marc Talbert. This book explores a year in the life of four contemporary teenage cowgirls as they live and work on their home ranches.*

El Parasol

1833 Cerrillos Road
(505) 995-8015

Breakfast Hours:
Monday-Friday 7am-11am,
Saturday, 8am-11am,
Sunday 9am-noon
Parking: Plentiful, but most folks just
drive through
Kid Component: *
Area: Cerrillos
Prices: $

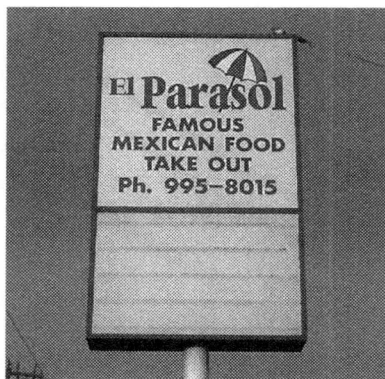

We know what you're thinking: Oh, no! Not another Cerrillos Road burrito joint!

Well, sort of. As the sign plainly states: "Famous Mexican Take-Out since 1958." Now, before you flip the page, let's analyze that description of El Parasol.

- Take-Out – here's your chance for a picnic, Santa Fe style. And you get to pick the location! Viewing the golden aspens, heading to the Opera Flea Market, trekking to a nearby pueblo, surprising your family with take-out for breakfast, or just treating your office-mates back in the break-room.

- Since 1958 – they've got staying power!

- Famous – word has definitely gotten out!

- Mexican – okay, burritos. But more, way more! ¡Pero mas, mucho mas!

Speaking of mas, let's consider masa, one of the main ingredients in tamales. El Parasol's tamales are handmade. In addition to the traditional pork filling, look for the daily specials. Green chile/chicken and vegetarian (filled with calabacitas) tie for the top spot in our list of favorites. When eating tamales, unless you really need extra fiber in your diet, always remove the corn husks! If you're a breakfast burrito lover, El Parasol will be near the top of your "best in town" list. But take note: everything on the menu is served all day except for the breakfast burritos! What this boils down to is that you have to

show up before 11:00 a.m. Monday through Saturday and by noon on Sunday to get in on the BBs. As long as we're talking about boiling, this might be a good opportunity to mention El Parasol's menudo (a soup made using tripe, hominy, and chile, stewed for hours with garlic and other spices). It comes by the pint or quart. Judging from the number of quarts we watched go out the door, this stuff is "better than Mamacita used to make!" Could that be because menudo is widely proclaimed to be an antidote for hangovers?

Other choices include tacos, burgers, burritos, combination plates, a foot long chili cheese dog and yes, Frito pie! Vegetarian offerings include tacos, burritos, quesadillas, and tostadas with optional guac (guacamole).

Getting back to El Parasol's Cerrillos Road location . . . it's always good to know where to find an umbrella in New Mexico, given the daily weather forecast: Chile Today, Hot Tamale!

Recommended reading: Despite the title of Gary Soto's book, we don't think you could ever have Too Many Tamales.

Eldorado Hotel - Eldorado Court

309 W. San Francisco Street
(505) 988-4455 (800) 955-4455

www.eldoradohotel.com

Breakfast Hours:
Monday-Saturday 6am-11:30am,
Sunday 6:30am-10am,
Sunday Brunch 11:30am-2pm
Kid Component: *
Parking: Valet guest parking in
underground garage, street and
municipal lots

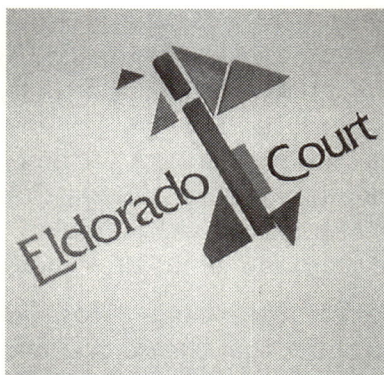

Area: Plaza
Prices: $$

If you feel like "going for the gold" for breakfast, you can't go wrong at the Eldorado Court. *En Español*, Eldorado means "the Golden One." We predict that after one taste of the Eldorado's traditional huevos rancheros, you'll know you've struck gold.

No, we didn't shout "Eureka!" – although that word describes our reaction after the first forkful from this colorful plate. We specified "Christmas" style (half red, half green) for the accompanying chile. The palette was completed with pink pinto beans, slices of green avocado, cream-colored potatoes O'Brien, and orange melted cheddar cheese. Peeking up through this delectable mouth-watering array were the golden huevos. A nice addition was the flour tortillas, tucked into their own covered warmer, which we immediately dubbed the "tortilla cozy."

There are plenty of gold nuggets buried in the Eldorado Court's breakfast menu. We loved the traditional brioche French toast, gilded with caramelized bananas, apple compote, and toasted pecans. In the same vein you can find old-fashioned buttermilk pancakes (topped with fresh berries, whipped cream, maple syrup and seasonal fruit) and Belgian waffles (topped with whipped cream, seasonal berries, maple syrup, and peanuts).

If you prefer the role of prospector, opt for the breakfast buffet and load up on your favorite food treasures. If you're looking to lighten your saddlebags, choose the spa breakfast (your choice of fruit juice

or frappé, egg whites any style with crispy tofu and sliced fruit or tomatoes). For a real grubstake, dig into the Eldorado signature steak and eggs.

Feeling creative? Create your own breakfast burrito! Starting with the basic tortilla and scrambled eggs, add your choice of: chorizo, ham, sausage, bacon, mushrooms, onions, tomatoes, grated jack cheese or goat cheese, topped with red or green chile and served with a potato torta. Similarly, you can also express yourself by creating your own breakfast omelet.

Extra golden touches at the Eldorado include fresh flowers on the tables and napkin rings in the shape of the prairie chicken (that bird is the hotel's logo). Contents of the breakfast buffet chafing dishes are written on small plates displayed above each one, and cloth napkins are tied to the handles, helping prevent those nasty steam burns that can happen when you lift the cover.

Don't depart the Eldorado Court without viewing the art. This is a huge room, and the art matches the scale of the space. Striking paintings feature gigantic cactus with sword-like spines. A super-sized snarling jaguar bares his sharp teeth and claws. Two enormous carved coyotes bay silently at the moon. Most striking is the animated sculpture of a coyote who seems to be singing the blues. His sidekicks, a pair of vultures perched on a saguaro cactus, a setting sun, and a yucca plant complete this moving picture.

Recommended reading: Coyote: A Trickster Tale from the American Southwest *told and illustrated by Gerald McDermott*

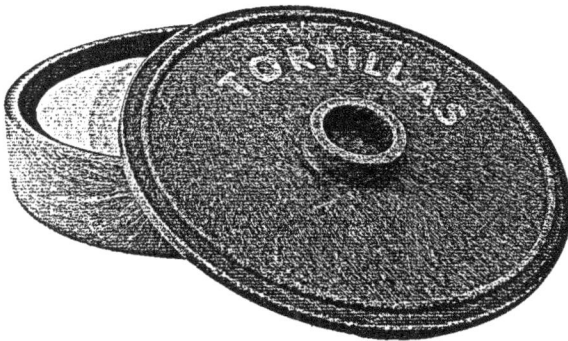

Farmers Market

Lot on the southwest corner at the intersection of Cerrillos Road and Guadalupe (market moves indoors to the Museo Cultural on Saturdays November-April)

(505) 983-4098

www.santafefarmersmarket.com

Breakfast Hours:
Tuesdays (May-October) 7am-noon,
Saturdays 7am-noon
Kid Component: **

Parking: Plentiful
Area: Cerrillos
Prices: $

When you hear the phrase "squash blossom," do you think of intricate turquoise and silver necklaces? If you come to the Santa Fe Farmers Market during the right time of year, there will be mounds of real squash blossoms displayed for sale. Squash blossoms are edible flowers, raw or cooked. A quick Internet search yields recipes using these bright yellow blossoms in salads, soups, frittatas, quesadillas, and more.

The phrase "eat in or take out" takes on a new meaning at the Farmers Market. Although you can certainly eat breakfast here, the main attraction is the incredible variety of food items that you can purchase to take home and whip up your very own breakfast, Santa Fe style.

At the booth called the Market Café, choose from burritos, stuffed croissants, tamales, pastries, muffins, and cookies (organic products provided by Cloud Cliff Bakery, proceeds help support the Farmers Market), and a variety of hot and cold drinks.

At the Intergalactic Food Company and Café booth, Mediterranean breads are made with 100% local organic flour and produce. A day's assortment might include the following spreads on a variety of breads: sun dried tomato/pesto, roasted garlic/fennel, apricot/rhubarb, and spinach/feta.

Resembling museum-quality still-life paintings, the artistic arrangements of huge oyster and winecap mushrooms in the "Desert Fungi"

booth took our breath away. Thanks to a tabletop propane stove, freshly sautéed samples were available at the tip of a toothpick. The mushrooms are grown in Llano, New Mexico, but you can grow your own by purchasing a mushroom growing kit at this booth. On another visit, different varieties of mushrooms were available: Lion's Mane and the exotic/erotic-looking Love Oysters. Many of the vendors provide samples of their wares, so it's possible to graze your way through all the stands without spending a dime for breakfast. Even if your plan is to come and eat samples, we bet you'll end up purchasing something to eat immediately in addition to fresh foods to take home. One taste of the organic raspberry red chile jam on a Wheat Thin® will have you reaching for your wallet.

Besides squash blossoms, a fantastic selection of cut flowers provides a feast for the eyes and nose. Non-edibles include sage bundles, lavender, organic soap, baskets, Indian corn, and dried arrangements. Here's a partial list of edible items you might see on any given day: squash, sprouts, garlic, cheese, fennel, baby carrots, apples, onions, chile, radishes, peaches, leeks, okra, apricots, tomatoes, basil, shallots, "greens for kitty," eggs "from cage free happy hens," icy cold apple cider, packages of dried chile (powdered, ground, crushed), dried blue corn (posole, meal), and all kinds of dried beans and soup mixes. The assortment of food changes from week to week.

This is one instance when we suggest that you read the "Recommended reading" title before visiting the location. Compile a list from the recipe at the end of the book and then come to the Farmers Market for fresh-from-the-field ingredients!

Recommended reading: Carlos learns the hard way what can happen if you don't wash your ears in Carlos and the Squash Plant/Carlos y la planta de calabaza *by Jan Romero Stevens. Included is a recipe for calabacitas.*

Felipe's Tacos

1711 Llano St.
(505) 473-9397

Breakfast Hours:
Monday-Saturday 9am-11am
Kid Component: **
Parking: Plentiful
Area: Midtown
Prices: $

As we drive and walk to breakfast restaurants in Santa Fe, we like to take note of some of the important landmarks in the city. Since we are both librarians, we take special note of Santa Fe's libraries. Felipe's Tacos sits just down the street from Santa Fe Public Library's busy branch, the La Farge Public Library. The library is named after Oliver La Farge, an anthropologist and writer.

Just like the La Farge Public Library, Felipe's Tacos is named after a person, Chef Felipe Martinez. You wouldn't guess it by its name, but Felipe's Tacos is one of Santa Fe's best stops for burritos in the morning. This restaurant has a fairly short time window for serving breakfast, but if you can escape from work for just a few midmorning minutes, you will come back to work a happy person with a hefty breakfast burrito in hand. According to the menu, Felipe's is "Health Conscious For You!" Felipe's does not deep-fry any foods or use lard in cooking. So when you want to go out for breakfast every single day, where could there be a healthier place to go?

The breakfast menu at Felipe's is short, but great. Felipe's puts together two breakfast burritos. The scrambled egg burrito automatically comes with bacon, and the chorizo and egg burrito speaks for itself. We love the burritos at this fast food Mexican restaurant. They are handheld burritos wrapped in soft flour tortillas and filled with lots of eggs. You won't be asked the traditional question "red or green?" at Felipe's because this restaurant has a salsa bar for breakfast and lunch. Once you have placed your order at the counter, venture over to the salsa bar and choose a topping. Choices include pico de gallo, red chile, onions, radishes, limes, or cilantro. If you can't limit yourself to one topping, try a little of everything! Soon after spooning your salsa

selections into miniature tubs, your order number will be called.

The restaurant has indoor and outdoor seating. Both areas are basic, with the outdoor seating being along side the restaurant's parking lot. We recommend either taking your heavy burrito back to work with you, or taking a seat at one of the tables. We have experienced many a mishap when trying to eat these juicy burritos while driving. Stained clothes and smelling like garlic and onion all day are just a few minor problems. Fender benders and other auto inconveniences are also likely, so eat these tasty burritos while sitting still.

The burritos are beautiful, but we also like the breakfast torta (a breakfast sandwich served on a homemade bun, filled with eggs, refried beans, and salsa). The torta is a messy finger-licking breakfast, so grab a fork and a pile of napkins.

If you aren't hungry between 9:00 a.m. and 11:00 a.m., definitely stop in for one of Felipe's Tacos' great drinks (no coffee). The freshly squeezed limeade is a perfect sweet drink, even for breakfast. You also have the option of choosing horchata with your breakfast. Horchata is a sweet milky Mexican drink made with rice, almond, cinnamon, and sugar.

Recommended reading: Oliver La Farge's books are available at the public library. Check out his Pulitzer Prize-winning first novel, Laughing Boy: A Navajo Love Story *or his collection of essays,* Behind the Mountains.

Flying Tortilla

4250-D Cerrillos Road
(505) 424-1680

Breakfast Hours:
Monday-Friday 6:30am-3pm,
Saturday 6:30am-3pm,
Sunday 7am-3pm
Kid Component: ***
Parking: Plentiful
Area: Cerrillos
Prices: $

It's a bird, it's a plane . . . no it's a flying tortilla! Flying tortillas bring to mind many imaginative visions: tortillas with snow white wings, tortillas flung across the table in the heat of a grand debate, tortilla dough spinning through the air before landing on a hot cook top. The staff at this restaurant has assured us that no tortillas have flown in this building, but the thought of going to the Flying Tortilla for breakfast in the morning may get you flying out of bed.

As you will learn later in this breakfast guide, Santa Fe's Pantry has been one of our favorite restaurants for years. We were thrilled when the Pantry's sister restaurant, Flying Tortilla, opened on Santa Fe's south side in late 2005. Not only is the location closer to our homes, it is a spacious restaurant with plenty of seating. Flying Tortilla, however, is following in its sister's footsteps, and you may have to wait outside for a table on busy weekend mornings.

Just because this restaurant is large and spacious, doesn't mean it isn't hopping with activity. On a recent midweek visit we spent nearly two hours chatting and enjoying our breakfast while watching the hustle and bustle of this new restaurant. Our coffee cups were never empty while we watched National Guard personnel dine on giant omelets, pancakes, and French toast; a woman escort her elderly father to a table and enjoy hot tea, corned beef, and eggs; and a construction worker sit alone at the community table eating a breakfast burrito.

We also enjoyed the breakfast burrito with the Egg Beaters© option, served with the same excellent red chile flavored potatoes found at the Pantry. Our dining companion designed her own breakfast

sandwich which included scrambled eggs, bacon, and cheese all wrapped in a low carb tortilla with a bowl of fruit on the side.

The Flying Tortilla is a great place for extended family group meals or meetings with co-workers. The front of the restaurant is devoted to a sizable dining room that can be closed off from the restaurant's large main room, allowing for private family banter and lively collegial discussions.

The Flying Tortilla's south side location also allows Albuquerque drivers easy access to great food on the way in to town. Commuters will not be disappointed with any of these meals picked up on-the-go.

The word is out: Flying Tortilla is fast on its way to becoming a new local favorite.

Recommended reading: In The Runaway Tortilla *by Eric A. Kimmel a tortilla runs away from a woman who is about to cook him. In this southwestern version of* The Gingerbread Man, *the tortilla is chased by Tía Lupe and Tío José, two horned toads, three donkeys, four jackrabbits, five rattlesnakes, and six buckaroos.*

French Pastry Shop & Crêperie – La Fonda Hotel

100 East San Francisco Street
(505) 983-6697

Breakfast Hours:
Daily 6:30am-5pm
Kid Component: *
Parking: La Fonda parking garage
has covered parking, fee charged;
street and municipal lots

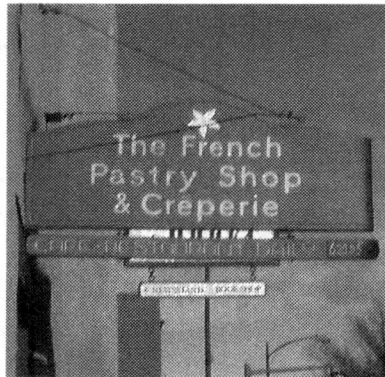

Area: Plaza
Prices: $$

Everyone knows the tale of Cinderella. Can your mind's eye visualize what the fireplace in the story looked like? We're willing to bet that your mental picture would be an exact match with the fantastic fireplace in this charming little restaurant.

You can enter the Crêperie two ways: from inside the La Fonda Hotel or from San Francisco Street. Sixteen round and square tables and a full complement of chairs are arranged in a very small area, so it's easy and fun to overhear what your neighbors are choosing from the menus posted on the walls and blackboards. Our favorite eavesdropping experience involved a youngster who expressed dismay at "nothing but French food!" We realized he was a Harry Potter fan when he suddenly exclaimed "Hey! Quiche has lots of the same letters as Quidditch!" He ordered accordingly, and voiced satisfaction with his choice.

In addition to quiche (both spinach and lorraine), we watched several plates of tourte milanese go by. According to our server, this is a variation of quiche containing spinach, roasted red peppers, ham, Swiss cheese, and egg, plus a top crust.

Crêpes are available in a wide variety, either as a meal or as a dessert. Our favorite meal crêpe has a ratatouille filling: zucchini, eggplant, tomatoes, onion, and green pepper. Dessert crêpes can be constructed with fruit and/or whipped cream or ice cream, or even Nutella! Tantalizing Croque Monsieur and Croque Madame hot sandwiches

include ham, cheese, and Béchamel sauce. *Naturellement*, Madame has an egg on top!

The huge fireplace mantel and surrounding dark brick wall provide an excellent backdrop for shiny brass and copper cooking utensils and a large rooster. In contrast are the colorful painted tinwork light fixtures. Bright yellow curtains frame the windows that look out onto busy San Francisco Street, where a seemingly endless number of people are snapping photographs of nearby St. Francis Cathedral.

Assorted signs advise the customers that "All pastries and breads are made on the premises" and "All pastries are made with pure butter and made fresh daily." The pastries in the display case are edible works of art. If you happen to need a loaf of bread shaped like an animal, choose from an alligator, a turtle, or a frog. We resisted the temptation to ask the pastry chef "Does the frog bread croak, Monsieur?"

Recommended reading: Little Gold Star/Estrellita de oro: A Cinderella Cuento retold in English and Spanish by Joe Hayes.

Garduño's Restaurant

130 Lincoln Place
(505) 983-9797

*http://www.gardunosrestaurants.
com*

Breakfast Hours:
Sundays 10:30am-3pm
Kid Component: ***
Parking: Paid behind building, will
validate for 1.5 hours. Street and
municipal lots

Area: Plaza
Prices: $$$

To go to Garduño's for brunch, you will have to follow the
breadcrumbs left by the late night cantina drinkers from Saturday
night. If you aren't finding the breadcrumbs, here are some hints:
Find Lincoln Place on Lincoln Avenue, a few blocks north of the
Plaza. Look for a hidden escalator in Lincoln Place. Ride the escalator
to the second floor of Lincoln Place and you will be at Garduño's'
large front door.

Garduño's is a New Mexico chain and a local favorite. Santa Fe's
Garduño's is a restaurant built for large parties, so if you and 50 of
your closest friends need a Sunday brunch hideaway, Garduño's is
you dream location. While the cavernous restaurant allows for large
parties, the smaller front room cantina is a comfortable place for solo
diners and smaller groups.

Garduño's' brunch buffet tables are long, loaded, and full of options.
You can request an omelet made to order, or dive into the wide
variety of sweet breakfasts, fruits, and Mexican foods. One section
of the buffet suggests diners should top the steamy French toast with
cherries, apples, or warm syrup. Green salads and a tray piled high
with fresh fruit welcomes health minded eaters. Mexican breakfast
options include firm scrambled eggs with green chile, potatoes with
red chile (potatoes adovada), and beef fajitas. Large slices of bacon
and sausage links complement every breakfast option.

A Sunday brunch wouldn't be complete without an outrageous
dessert. Once your brunch plate is empty, venture back to the buffet

for chocolate dipped strawberries, cinnamon sprinkled flan, or tapioca pudding served in a parfait glass.

Cantina drinks start to flow at noon on Sunday.

If you miss Santa Fe's downtown Garduño's, you will have a second chance to catch this great New Mexico cuisine as you leave our fair state. The Albuquerque Sunport also houses a Garduño's Restaurant where breakfast is served daily with a buffet option from 6:00 a.m. to 10:00 a.m.

Recommended reading: For information on Garduño's' nightlife and other Santa Fe late night adventures, check out Bob Eggers' Santa Fe After Dark: An Illustrated Guide.

Guadalupe Café

442 Old Santa Fe Trail
(505) 982-9762

Breakfast Hours:
Tuesday-Friday 7am-11am,
Saturday-Sunday 8am-2pm
Kid Component: *
Parking: Limited parking behind
restaurant; street and municipal lots
Area: Plaza
Prices: $$

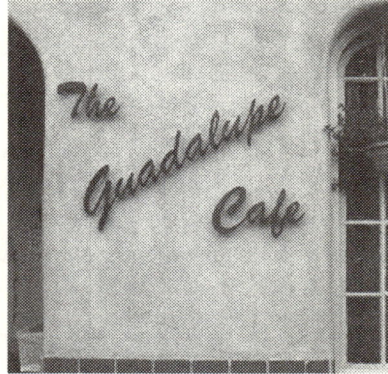

The Guadalupe Café is a favorite restaurant for locals and tourists. If you find yourself near the Plaza, it's a short walk to some of the best breakfast food in the state. Diners approaching the café will be treated to brick flower-lined walkways and views of the New Mexico state capitol building. The fare is New Mexican cuisine with a gourmet twist. While the menu is filled with tempting delectables, we recommend ordering from the restaurant's specials (specials are posted right inside the door).

If you decide to order off the menu, you will have a pleasing selection of food options. Entrees include blue corn piñon nut breaded French toast and Florentine egg rolls made with spinach, feta cheese, and scrambled eggs in a whole-wheat tortilla. Vegetarians and non-egg eaters will find extensive and unexpected dining options such as the exquisite breakfast burrito, a burrito filled with spinach and mushrooms topped with cheese and chile.

On weekdays, diners will find a sleepy morning café. If you are planning on eating breakfast on a weekend, arrive early or be prepared for a substantial wait. The people-watching at the Guadalupe Café is superb, so waiting time passes quickly.

The restaurant's seating is cozy and includes café chairs mixed with bench seating. On most visits, the mixture of tastes and smells causes you to forget the close quarters. In warmer seasons, diners may choose outdoor seating under large umbrellas. Several outdoor tables include views of the café's next-door neighbor, the New Mexico state capitol building, familiarly known as the Round House.

Recommended reading: In Michael McGarrity's Serpent Gate, *former police detective Kevin Kerney finds himself inside the New Mexico state capitol building investigating an art heist from the Governor's Gallery.*

Harry's Roadhouse

Old 96 Las Vegas Highway
(505) 989-4629

Breakfast Hours:
Monday-Friday 7am-11am,
Saturday 7am-noon,
Sunday 7am-1pm
Kid Component: ***
Parking: Plentiful
Area: East of Santa Fe
Prices: $$

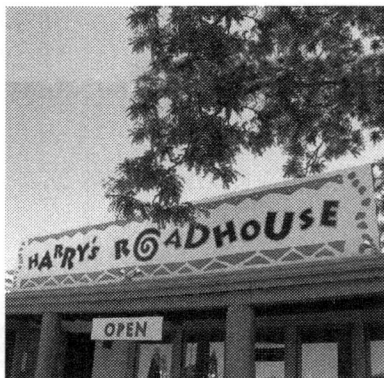

Roadhouses conjure up visions of dirty cross-country travelers and rough and tumble biker gangs. You may experience an element of this rough road life as you negotiate the parking lot at Harry's Roadhouse, but once you have made it through the front door of this roadhouse, you will find a quirky, elegant, and charming restaurant you will want to come back to time and time again.

Harry's Roadhouse is a longtime favorite restaurant for Santa Feans and folks living in the hills outside Santa Fe. If you visit Harry's on a weekend morning, you may find a bit of a wait for a table, but there is comfortable waiting room seating both inside and outside.

The interior of Harry's Roadhouse has two distinct seating options. If you are seated in the dining room to the right of the front door, you will experience a 1950s diner. The room is replete with linoleum floors, Formica tables, and a short lunch counter. Pastel padded bar stools add the finishing touch to this mid-century dining room. The two other dining rooms at Harry's are more reminiscent of an elegant Santa Fe café. These rooms have brick floors, plaster walls, wood tables and chairs, and they are decorated with photographs by local artists.

No matter where you are seated, you will soon find that the primary reason this restaurant has been a local favorite is the consistently great food that spills through the kitchen doors. You can review the menu for your breakfast selections or look at the daily specials posted on boards throughout the restaurant. If you are lucky, the daily specials might include lemon ricotta pancakes with strawberries.

We splurged on the daily pan fried trout special. This dish comes with a beautiful tasty corn breaded trout, eggs any way you want them, super seasoned fried potatoes, and homemade toast. We also enjoyed Harry's breakfast burrito. It is a traditional New Mexico breakfast burrito served with fried potatoes.

Breakfast breads are abundant at Harry's and all of the tables include a large jar of strawberry preserves, which we lavishly spread on the toasty breads. Given the option, we would have sat all afternoon at Harry's eating toasted bread smothered with strawberry preserves. While we enjoyed every bite of our meal, the freshly made chocolate éclairs sat expectantly on the lunch counter in the 1950s room of the diner. Since breakfast will probably fill you to the brim, consider taking home an éclair for a mid afternoon sweet snack.

Kids will enjoy Harry's just as much as adults. Children have their own menu and receive a coloring picture and crayons just for bringing their parents to this high-class roadhouse that sits just moments outside of Santa Fe's city limits.

Recommended reading: The pan fried trout at Harry's Roadhouse made us think about fishing for our very own breakfast trout, and it might make you consider a similar adventure. Ti Piper's book Fishing in New Mexico *might be a good start for your hunt for the perfect stream.*

Hilton of Santa Fe – Chamisa Courtyard Café

100 Sandoval Street
(505) 988-2811 (800) 336-3676

www.hiltonofsantafe.com

Breakfast Hours:
Monday-Saturday 6:30-11am,
Sunday 6:30am-2pm
Kid Component: *
Parking: Guest parking lot, street and
municipal lots

Area: Plaza
Prices: $$

"Those are the longest ristras I've ever seen!" and "They'd make the Guinness Book of World Records for sure!" were just two of the comments we overheard walking into the Hilton for breakfast one morning. We wove our way through a family group snapping pictures and marveling over the red chile ristras (strings of dried red chile peppers) hanging near the main entrance. Probably measuring at least 12 feet, they're suspended from the lovely portal.

Past the ristras and through the door, take a right and head through the faux-stone flower-bedecked archway. Follow the hall to the Chamisa Courtyard Café, which was once an open courtyard in the Ortiz hacienda, an historic homestead of one of Santa Fe's most prominent early families.

The light-filled courtyard with a lovely fountain in the center gives the impression of outdoor dining, thanks to enormous skylights. Comfortable chairs with woven backs look like they're crafted out of tree branches with the twigs trimmed off. Plenty of potted plants and sapphire-blue hanging pots containing cascading vines and flowers add to the alfresco ambience. Did we say fresco? Adorning the walls of the Courtyard Café are frescoes by Native American artist Randy Lee White.

Breakfast is served daily with a full menu and buffet. A special buffet brunch is served exclusively on Sundays. Our breakfast burrito buddy was totally satisfied with his burrito, which came with hash browns,

black beans, and lots of green chile and cheese, and was almost too much for one meal. Other menu choices include blue and yellow corn pancakes (the yellow comes from yellow corn kernels), buttermilk pancakes, Belgian waffles, and French toast. A variety of egg dishes are available, including Santa Fe style eggs (blue corn cakes, two eggs any style, fresh picante, black bean galletas, and fresh fruit salsa). Whenever we visit the Hilton, some folks in our party opt for the breakfast buffet, and express delight at the variety of offerings. The fresh fruit array is almost too beautiful to disturb, but our artist friend composed an edible still life on her plate, which soon became only a memory.

We have to admire the determination of the self-described "health nut" in our group who chose the light and lean breakfast (Egg Beaters®, turkey sausage or lean bacon, cottage cheese, and fresh fruit), and didn't even ask for a taste of our yummy muffin.

Although breakfast at the Hilton is delicious anytime, the hotel really outdoes itself on special holiday buffets. The Thanksgiving offering is outstanding, and usually sells out in advance.

Recommended reading: As they prepare to make chile ristras, a young girl hears the story of how magical chile seeds given to her great grandfather, a farmer in the hills of New Mexico, ensured the continuation of the chile pepper in Chiles for Benito/Chiles para Benito *by New Mexico author Ana Baca.*

Horseman's Haven Café

4354 Cerrillos Road
(505) 471-5420

Breakfast Hours:
Monday-Saturday 8am-8pm,
Sunday 8:30am-2pm
Kid Component: **
Parking: Plentiful but sometimes a bit
crowded
Area: Cerrillos

Prices: $

When the waitress says "red or green?" and follows up right away with "The green is hotter!" . . . *trust her*! Especially if you're not fully awake.

Horseman's Haven's breakfast burrito (two scrambled eggs, two strips of bacon topped with chile and melted cheese, served with home fries) is a classic. Smothered with red, it's plenty hot. You'd think the Fire Marshall would put a ban on anything hotter, considering the restaurant's location so close to a gas station. Okay, you might not actually see the Fire Marshall here, but if the parking lot is any indication, the place seems to be a favorite of the State Police (and it's probably not just because their headquarters are just down the street).

A sure-fire (sorry, couldn't resist) indicator of perfection in the hotness of chile is the need for tissues. If your eyes water after the first couple bites, and you're wiping away tears of joy . . . that's perfection, and it's here. Perfection of another kind can be experienced in the Horseman's Haven's home fries. They're made of pure potatoes (no onion, bacon, chile, nothing but spuds!) with the exact amount of butter flavor to deliver yet another taste bud triumph.

Horseman's Haven rounds up the usual suspects for breakfast: huevos rancheros, omelets, pancakes, French toast, carne adovada, chorizo, steak and eggs, and so forth. As it says right at the top of the menu, "Bienvenidos: New Mexican style cooking—Como en su casa." If people cooked this well at home, this place wouldn't be nearly as packed as it is.

Then there's the décor. It's a haven for horsemen all right, from the silhouettes of cowboys in action to the long horns mounted over the window between the counter and the kitchen. Naturally there's a portrait of John Wayne, plus a reproduction of the movie poster for "Hondo," starring The Duke. A ristra of red, green, yellow, and purple chile lights twinkles on one wall.

The stools at the counter can accommodate ten people, otherwise booths and tables are available. In addition, there are two massive curved corner banquettes providing spacious yet cozy areas for groups of six or so. The 8:00 a.m. opening (8:30 a.m. on weekends) is a drawback for early birds and folks wanting to swing by on the way to work. Once the place is open, though, the restaurant bursts with people. Remember, takeout is available.

Yet another phrase found on the menu is "Ojalá! you enjoy your comida" which loosely translates to "Here's hoping/let's hope you enjoy your meal." The cooks and staff seem eager to make sure that happens.

Recommended reading: Buster Burro thinks that men wear bandana scarves in order to keep their whiskers out of their beans in Tony Hillerman's kid-friendly Buster Mesquite's Cowboy Band, *illustrated by Ernest Franklin.*

Hotel Santa Fe – Amaya

1501 Paseo de Peralta
(505) 982-1200

www.hotelsantafe.com/dining/index.html

Breakfast Hours:
Monday-Friday 7am-10am,
Saturday-Sunday 7am-11am
Kid Component: **
Parking: Plentiful

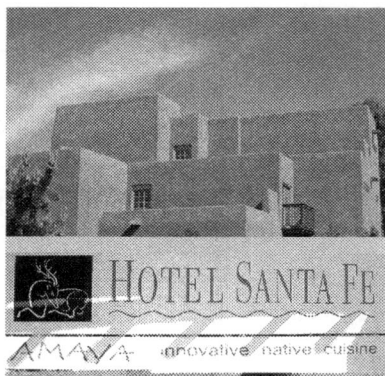

Area: Plaza
Prices: $$

We sit quietly on wooden benches in our teepee, shaded from the harsh sun. A thin coyote runs past the entrance of our desert dwelling, and in the distance a hawk cries. Dry winds quietly whip the teepee's canvas walls as we anxiously await our far-traveling guests. As we hear our guests approach, we cry "Mah-wann, Mah-wann" (meaning "welcome" in the language of the Picuris people).

Okay, so maybe the coyote was a dream and the hawk cry occurred later in the day, but if you have ever fantasized about spending some time in a teepee, the Amaya at the Hotel Santa Fe should be on your "must visit" list of restaurants.

The people of Picuris Pueblo in northern New Mexico own the Hotel Santa Fe and its fabulous restaurant, the Amaya. The modern pueblo style hotel provides comfortable spaces for eating and relaxation, including a 22-foot teepee in the restaurant's courtyard. The teepee can be reserved for groups and special events. If the teepee is not reserved during your visit, a quick sit inside the canvas structure will allow even the most serious adult some quiet time of peaceful contemplation.

Along with providing a unique dining experience, the Amaya is also focused on outstanding elegant dining. Inside seating is available during the colder months, but we recommend the outside seating options whenever space is available. The brick patio is shaded by a portal and big table umbrellas. The courtyard flows into a lawn and flower garden. Birds and sculptures find their home in this peaceful

yard. Patio diners sit at large sturdy stone tables in relaxing padded chairs and enjoy the remarkably quiet atmosphere of this city-center restaurant.

For breakfast, you have your choice of eating from the full buffet or ordering off the breakfast menu. Buffet items include toasts, cereals, pastries, and yogurt. The buffet may be best for someone who has astonishingly grown tired of New Mexico's cuisine, but we recommend the menu items.

Chefs at the Amaya work with traditional Native American ingredients to create modern breakfast dishes. During our breakfast, we enjoyed the chilaquiles (soft thick corn tortilla strips topped with eggs, cheese, and red or green chile). The dish came with a side of grilled potatoes and pinto beans, both of which were slightly sweet. The sweetness was the perfect touch for breakfast.

We also liked the Amaya's perfectly sized breakfast burrito. We have found some breakfast burritos in Santa Fe to be too big, and near the end of the meal, they become burdensome. This burrito, however, was filled with flavor and neither left us wanting more nor feeling too full.

Recommended reading: John P. Harrington has compiled stories from Rosendo Vargas of Picurís Pueblo and published them in Indian Tales from Picurís Pueblo.

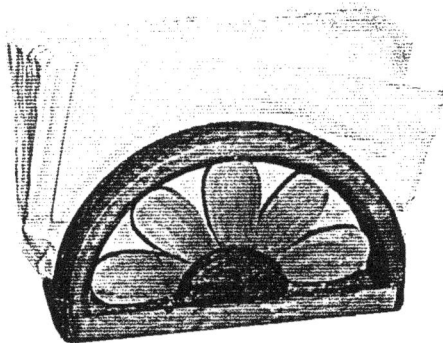

Inn and Spa of Loretto – Baleen

211 Old Santa Fe Trail
(505) 984-7915

www.hotelloretto.com/dining.cfm

Breakfast Hours:
Monday-Saturday 7am-11am,
Sunday Brunch 7am-2pm
Kid Component: *
Parking: Valet parking, street and
municipal lots

Area: Plaza
Prices: $$$

The Baleen is true sophistication in breakfast dining. It's tucked into the beautiful downtown hotel, the Inn and Spa at Loretto. Baleen's dining rooms have an updated elegant Santa Fe feel, with colorful modern wooden sculptures adorning the rooms' nichos. The two dining rooms are filled with large tables and soft black leather cushioned chairs. Every table is covered in a thick white tablecloth with a potted plant in the center. Some of the best seats in the house include tables by the windows looking out on to the Loretto Chapel. There are also very private booths with bench seating on three sides.

The menu is a pleasure to behold. Dishes range from apple pecan French toast to red chili rubbed breakfast steak. Other options include ordering your own omelet with your choice of ingredients, or trusting the skilled chefs with the chaco omelet (made with green chile, chorizo, and cheese). Drinks include freshly squeezed juices, Bloody Marys, and mimosas.

Our breakfasts at Baleen were so amazing, we thought about them all day. The crab cake Benedict was both beautiful and delicious. The layered dish starts off with a soft English muffin topped with a thin layer of spinach, a soft thick crab cake, and eggs Benedict with a creamy hollandaise sauce. The crab cakes were perfectly cooked so that they began to fall apart with the slightest encouragement of a fork. The cakes were sparingly filled with corn and red pepper, all lightly flavored with lemon. Every layer of the crab cake Benedict called to be tasted individually before indulging in a full bite. A perfect, tender,

inch-thick hash brown cake complemented the complex flavors in the entrée.

We also highly recommend Baleen's breakfast burrito. Even if you are very hungry when you come to eat, you may have to leave some of the breakfast burrito behind. This burrito is a gourmet version of Santa Fe's traditional breakfast delight. The burrito comes filled with egg, a sparingly used tomato sauce, black beans, bacon, chorizo, and hash browns. The burrito is topped with cheese and a mild green chile sauce.

After you have finished eating and the dishes have been removed, take a moment to enjoy the last of your coffee and sink in to this quiet moment before moving on with your day. See the small birds jumping around the fountain in the courtyard. Smell the sweet aromas of the fruit pancakes being delivered to a neighboring table. Hear a grandmother and granddaughter talk about their train ride to Lamy. Feel absolutely content.

After breakfast, take a short stroll through the Inn and Spa of Loretto's hallway to the Loretto Chapel. The Loretto Chapel is a dainty Gothic revival-style chapel built for the Sisters of Loretto. The chapel is known for its miraculous staircase.

Recommended reading: Alice Bullock explores some of the Loretto Chapel's mysteries in her book Loretto and the Miraculous Staircase. *For light fiction reading about the staircase's origins, pick up* The Staircase *by Ann Rinaldi.*

Inn of the Anasazi – Anasazi Restaurant

113 Washington Avenue
(505) 988-3236

*www.innoftheanasazi.com/pages/
restaurant.html*

Breakfast Hours:
Daily 7am-10:30am
Kid Component: *
Parking: Garage parking for guests,
street and municipal lots

Area: Plaza
Prices: $$$

Anasazi has been translated to mean "ancient stranger," "ancient enemy," or "ancient one." The translation for the Inn of the Anasazi Restaurant might be "ancient luxury." Viewing the Inn from the outside, you see a two story brown pueblo style building. As you step inside, your surroundings shrink. The ceilings are low masses constructed using large tree vigas, dark wood floors are beneath your feet, and the smell of brewing coffee pulls you through the small bar area into the breakfast dining room. Walls throughout the restaurant are either warm plaster coated or flat ancient stone. Tables are dressed in thick tablecloths. Elegant napkins sit folded at each place setting, and the tables have black and white ceramic flower vases, sugar bowls, and salt and pepper shakers. The walls are lined with banco seating (bench seating attached to the wall), and large wooden chairs comfortably seat breakfasters.

Soon after you arrive at your table, a server will bring you coffee, tea, or freshly squeezed orange juice. Coffee is served in oversized black and white mugs, with a matching oversized ceramic creamer. Tea arrives at the table in a tall glass infuser. Orange juice is served in large, tall, stemmed glasses.

The spiral symbol is commonly found in ancient petroglyphs and is used throughout the Inn of the Anasazi Restaurant. Spirals adorn the wait staffs' bolo ties, the bottom of the coffee cups, and the walls along the southeast side of the restaurant. The spiral's actual ancient specific meaning has never been identified, but many believe the

symbol represents emergence from the underworld or migration.

Migrating from the dining room to the restrooms below the restaurant is a descent into an underworld. The narrow stairs take you down to another world with even lower ceilings and darker wood. The knots in the wood of the bathroom stalls look like owl eyes peeking at you while you are alone in the deep recesses of the inn. The mood lightens as you exit the bathroom, climb back up the stone stairs, and return to your table.

The dining room atmosphere is soothing, and comfort food pours out of the kitchen at the Inn. Menu items include sweet treats such as scones, cinnamon rolls, and blueberry flapjacks with almond-maple syrup. We ordered the brioche French toast with raspberry, mango, and maple syrup and were in awe when it arrived. The French toast was cut into strips two inches thick and about five inches long, and geometrically piled in the center of the plate. The three syrups were gracefully drizzled over the toast making for a sweet (but not too sweet) breakfast extravaganza.

Egg dishes include the soft scrambled egg and bacon quesadilla with pico de gallo and guacamole and a three egg omelet to which you can add your own selection of ingredients. The choice of fillings includes ham, avocado, mushrooms, green chile or tomato, and white cheddar or asadero cheese. The omelet is accompanied by green chile hash browns, a treat all by themselves!

Recommended reading: For many years, the people living in New Mexico's Chaco Canyon were referred to as Anasazi; scholars now talk about the Chaco Canyon dwellers as Puebloan people. Mark A. Taylor is the author of a fictional novel, Chaco: A Tale of Ancient Lives, *about the life and demise of Chaco Canyon as seen through the eyes of two young boys.*

La Fonda Hotel – La Plazuela

100 E. San Francisco St.
(505) 982-5511 (800) 523-5002

www.lafondasantafe.com

Breakfast Hours:
Daily 7am–10:30am (except the
Saturday and Sunday of Indian
Market when they open at 6:30am)
Kid Component: ***
Parking: Pay to park in La Fonda's
enclosed garage, street and

municipal lots
Area: Plaza
Prices: $$

How did Lewis Carroll's Alice feel when she became very small and found herself in a garden of flowers? Probably much like we felt seated in La Fonda's jewel-box: La Plazuela. Live trees and potted palms grow in huge planters. Fresh flowers often grace the tables. The surrounding walls consist almost completely of over 400 hand-painted windows. If you're dining with kids, play "I Spy" to see if they can spot particular designs in the colorful windows, including butterflies, birds, swans, owls, fruit, rabbits, grasshoppers, and Zia signs, to name just a few.

Designs from some of the painted windows are used as a border on the menu. *Desayuno Speciales*/Breakfast Specialties include: La Fonda eggs Benedict (poached eggs on a toasted English muffin with Canadian bacon and grilled tomatillos, hollandaise sauce, and fresh cilantro); huevos oaxacas (three eggs scrambled with roasted tomato salsa, tostaditos, and poblana rajas); omelette Mexicana (three eggs with chorizo, onions, asadero cheese, and tomatillo salsa); southwestern burrito (a flour tortilla filled with scrambled eggs and choice of chorizo, pork sausage, or bacon, covered with red or green chile and topped with cheese); and of course, huevos rancheros. A special treat is truchas o bistek con huevos (grilled rainbow trout or rib eye steak with two eggs any style). All of the above are served with mix and match sides that include pinto or black beans, breakfast potatoes or posole, and toast, an English muffin, a bagel or tortillas.

If you have a taste for something sweet, choose from two kinds of

Belgian waffles (plain and banana pecan); French toast made with raisin pecan bread; and three types of pancakes (buttermilk, blueberry, or [our choice] blue corn piñon). We can testify that there is at least one piñon in every forkful!

Take your time to enjoy the lovely surroundings as you savor your meal. Flagstone floor, ristras, tall pillars topped with giant Indian pots, and murals add to the unique ambience. La Fonda is a place we've been experiencing since childhood, and it holds great memories for us. If, like Alice, you're "curiouser and curiouser" about this Santa Fe landmark, the research has already been done for you. There's a brief history of La Fonda on the breakfast menu. For further information on the hotel's history and art, pick up brochures on these topics at the front desk in the lobby. While there, don't miss the old fashioned telephone just to the right of the registration area. Exclusively for calling individual rooms in the hotel, this house phone looks like a genuine antique until you spot the small pushbuttons in the rotary dial. It's quite a curiosity for a generation growing up with cell phones.

As you exit the dining room, stop to look at the framed collection of historic photos of La Fonda on the pillar facing the entrance to La Plazuela. If you have time, take the stairway to your right. From the second floor you can look down into La Plazuela. Framed posters from past seasons of the Santa Fe Opera, Indian Market, Fiestas de Santa Fe, and other events line the balcony walls.

Your visit to La Fonda will stay with you for a long time. You may even dream that you've been in Wonderland.

Recommended reading: The harvesting and shucking of blue corn and the gathering of piñon nuts are beautifully described and illustrated by Jonathan Warm Day in his book Taos Pueblo: Painted Stories. *La Fonda's original interior designer was Mary Colter. To find out more about Colter and her other architectural masterpieces, pick up* Mary Colter: Architect of the Southwest *by Arnold Berke.*

La Posada de Santa Fe – El Fuego

300 Palace Avenue
(505) 986-0000

*www.laposada.rockresorts.com/info/
din.fuego.asp*

Breakfast Hours:
Daily 7am-11am,
Sunday Brunch 11:30am-2pm
Kid Component: **
Parking: Valet parking, street and
municipal lots

Area: Plaza
Prices: $$$

Elegant, romantic, luxurious, and simple. These are just a few words that describe the breakfast atmosphere at the La Posada de Santa Fe's El Fuego restaurant. The El Fuego is adjacent to the century-old Staab mansion on the La Posada's property. The mansion is a three-story brick French Empire-style home built in the 1880s by Santa Fe merchant, Abraham Staab. Abraham's wife, Julia Staab, is believed by some to haunt the mansion. While the mansion section of the hotel has maintained its old world charm, the La Posada property was completely renovated in 1998. It now stands as one of Santa Fe's most elegant hotel, spa, bar, and restaurant venues.

El Fuego has both indoor and outdoor seating. Eating inside you will find comfortable luxury as you sit in large oversized couches and chairs placed in front of dark wooden tables. A fireplace may warm the room with its glowing embers. Outside seating in warmer months is also an elegant dining pleasure. The dining courtyard is behind the Staab mansion, and is landscaped in a contemporary New Mexican style with a stone patio, outdoor fireplace, waterfalls, blooming flowers, and dainty aspen trees. The outdoor tables are large glass-topped tables with seating for as many as six people. White umbrellas shade breakfast diners from early morning rays. The tables are set with straw placemats and fresh flowers.

No matter what you order at El Fuego, it will look beautiful and taste heavenly. Entrées are served on pristine white china plates. During our dining extravaganza we savored the stuffed croissant French

toast, a soft breaded croissant filled with cream cheese served with maple syrup and perfectly prepared strips of bacon. We also found the southwestern omelet irresistible (filled with goat cheese, toasted chili, sun-dried tomatoes, ham, and avocado and topped with red or green chile). Served with breakfast potatoes and toast, it more than satisfied our avocado craving and definitely pushed the flavor envelope!

Other breakfast options include the sweet Hillsboro style waffles (topped with apple-cinnamon compote, maple syrup, cinnamon butter, and crème) and the duck egg and wild mushroom frittata (wild mushroom ragout, baby spinach, and red chile).

The elegant serving dishes charmed us. The butter came served upon a square glass plate, and the jam for our bread was served on a long rectangular glass plate with three indentations for three types of jam. We were thrilled to see the bill come to our table atop a large yellow square glass plate.

Recommended reading: Julia Staab's ghost isn't the only apparition in Santa Fe; many downtown historic buildings may have spirits, ghosts, or poltergeists. One of New Mexico's best collections of ghost stories is New Mexico Ghost Stories *by Antonio R. Garcez. Read about ghosts at some of our favorite downtown haunts including Canyon Road and La Residencia, right across the street from La Posada.*

Las Salsas

2400 Cerrillos Rd.
(505) 474-6542

Breakfast Hours:
Monday-Saturday 6am-11am,
Sunday Brunch 8am-2pm
Kid Component: ***
Parking: Plentiful
Area: Cerrillos
Prices: $$

Great New Mexican breakfast cuisine is fairly common in Santa Fe. Most restaurants serve a hearty New Mexican breakfast burrito, omelets filled with red and green chile, and huevos rancheros served with grilled potatoes and/or pinto beans. While Las Salsas has several New Mexican breakfast dishes, try to leave your New Mexican food expectations behind when you step into this restaurant. Here you will drop the "new" in New Mexican food, and be truly delighted by traditional Mexican cuisine.

Las Salsas is easy to find. It is the bright yellow building on Cerrillos just south of St. Michaels Drive. The building is newly remodeled and has nice wooden floors. Mexican artwork decorates the walls and guitar music echoes through the high-ceilinged eating space.

Las Salsas has a regular menu for breakfast Monday through Saturday. Menu items include huevos a la Mexicana (scrambled eggs with tomatoes, onions, and jalapeños, served with beans and potatoes cooked with chorizo) and huevos motuleños (two fresh corn tortillas served with ham, fried eggs, and spicy cheese served with beans and potatoes).

Because Las Salsas offers an opportunity to try Mexican foods not commonly found in New Mexico, we highly recommend the Sunday brunch buffet. There you can try many different dishes, and if you get a particular item that you don't especially like, your entire breakfast is not ruined. If, on the other hand, you find something outstanding, the buffet is only a couple of feet away and you can go back for a whole plate of your new-found favorite food.

At the buffet, everyone will recognize cereals, fruits, biscuits and gravy, and pastries. A chef at the head of the buffet awaits your omelet order. We tried almost everything. Mixed with the pastries we found Mexican sweet bread and cakes that we enjoyed as the not too sweet substitute for a cinnamon roll. Menudo and posole were ready to be ladled from steaming pots. Our favorite buffet item was the flavorful and not too spicy rajas, green chile strips in a cream and onion sauce. We also liked the molletes, a slice of baked bread topped with refried beans and cheese. Huevos ahogados were also served at the buffet, scrambled eggs mixed with onions, peppers, and salsa.

If you're in the mood for an exciting breakfast that is more than a giant breakfast burrito topped with chile, Las Salsas may be the start of a beautiful friendship.

Recommended reading: For a brief easy-to-read history of New Mexico, look for Marc Simmons' book, New Mexico: An Interpretive History.

Little Anita's

2811 Cerrillos Road
(505) 473-4505

http://www.littleanitas.com/index.
html

Breakfast Hours:
Daily 7am-1pm
Kid Component: ***
Parking: Plentiful
Area: Cerrillos
Prices: $$

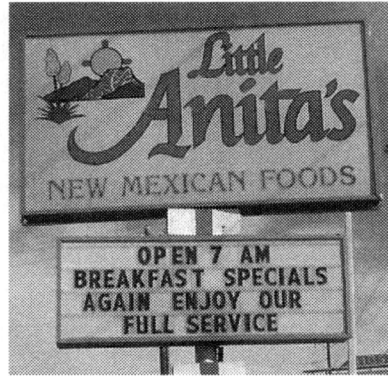

Little Anita's is perfect for a tasty, no-frills, relatively inexpensive place to eat some traditional New Mexican breakfast food. The restaurant is frequently filled with tourists, locals, people dining with their families, and individuals dining alone. On weekends the restaurant can get busy in the mid morning, but you will almost never have to wait in line. If you choose to dine-in on a weekday, you will have amazing service because the waitstaff will be serving only a handful of diners.

Little Anita's has recently been remodeled. Booths have been replaced with café chairs and tables. Brightly colored walls and large windows give the restaurant a warm ambiance. The restaurant is spacious and has brick floors, so it isn't always the quietest place to spend the morning, but the food is consistently good. Late morning diners will be served hot salsa with crispy fresh chips and hot sopapillas.

Everything on Little Anita's menu is great and will fill you up. The menu offers two breakfast burrito options: the breakfast burrito and the breakfast burrito grande. Both burritos come with two scrambled eggs wrapped in a flour tortilla topped with cheese and your choice of green and/or red chile and a side of hash browns. The breakfast burrito grande is bigger as the name implies, and includes chorizo, potatoes, and refried beans on the side. Both are examples of the quintessential New Mexican breakfast burritos.

We can also highly recommend any of the skillet options available. These entrées are served in a cast iron skillet atop a wooden board. Skillets include eggs any style, potatoes, green pepper, and chile

served with a choice of meats (ham, bacon, and chicken fried steak to name a few). For any egg meal, Egg Beaters® are available upon request.

Kids can order small portions of hotcakes, French toast, and/or eggs. For breakfast eaters who do not crave chile at every meal, adult portions of hotcakes, French toast, and eggs are also available. Side orders include sausage, bacon, hash browns, toast and English muffins.

Little Anita's also offers two items on the breakfast menu for carryout: a handheld breakfast burrito and huevos rancheros. The breakfast burritos are inexpensive and, for a small additional charge, potatoes, bacon, and/or chorizo may be added. Consider picking up an order of amazing breakfast burritos for your co-workers on the way to work! For fast service, call ahead for your breakfasts on the go.

Across the street from the restaurant, visitors will be happy to find a Santa Fe tourist destination: Jackalope Mercado (a shopping market that includes a prairie dog town, vendors selling jewelry, pottery and furniture imported from Mexico, and knick knacks from around the world). It is a short but very dangerous walk across heavy Cerrillos Road traffic to the Jackalope Mercado. We recommend you enjoy your breakfast and then drive to the shopping menagerie.

Recommended reading: Children will enjoy a book featuring the southwest's mythical horned rabbit, the jackalope. Janet Stevens and Susan Stevens Crummel's book, Jackalope, *begins with a rabbit's wish to be scary-looking.*

Los Potrillos

947 Cerrillos Road
(505) 992-0550

Breakfast Hours:
Daily 8am-12pm
Kid Component: ***
Parking: Plentiful
Area: Cerrillos
Prices: $$

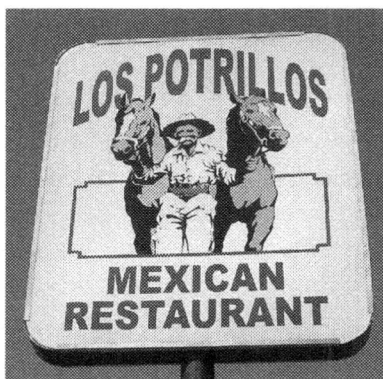

Restaurants in Santa Fe have to be good. The competition is so fierce, if a place is dishing out mediocre food, it isn't going to last. Los Potrillos is one of Santa Fe's newest restaurants and we predict it's here for the long haul.

While the outside of the restaurant looks like a traditional pizzeria, remember the old saying about judging books. Ignore the building's cover, and be prepared to be seated in one of the most relaxing Mexican restaurants in the city. In English, "los potrillos" means "the colts" and the restaurant's decorators have tastefully created a modern Mexican horse restaurant. The subdued colors give the interior an elegant feel, yet so many of the decorative touches are fun for both adults and children. During one of our visits, a little girl ran into the restaurant crying to her brother, "I get to sit next to the pony!" She dashed over to the large family-sized booth and snuggled up to a wooden sculpture of a tiny colt.

The chairs are the most stunning feature of Los Potrillos' décor. Each chair is a work of art. Large blonde wood chairs fill the restaurant's center area. Each has a horse head carved into the back. The walls are decorated with cowboy hats, horseshoes, leather chaps, and saddles. Iron lamps hang from the ceiling. Tabletops are colorfully painted with village scenes and burlap curtains hang from the windows. Large booths line the restaurant walls and are upholstered with soft brown vinyl. The back wall is a painted landscape with cowboys riding their horses through a Mexican village.

After sitting down, the waitperson will hand you a large menu

and you will need several long moments to review each item's description. While you read, gigantic glasses filled with the drink of your choice will be brought to your table. The first pages of the menu explain Los Potrillos' dining philosophy, "Los Potrillos is dedicated to rescue the recipes that Mexican women have produced in such a rich culinary style. Enjoy our breakfast dishes that are cooked homestyle while you are surrounded by a very pleasant Mexican country style environment."

The menu offers many egg options. On our first visit, we ordered huevos los potrillos (a corn tortilla quesadilla smothered with tomatillo sauce and topped with eggs any way you like). It was a wonderful mixture of flavors, unlike any other breakfast in town. We also ordered huevos coporal (two fried eggs served with chile pasado). The side of chile consisted of green chile peppers fried with onions and tomatoes. The flavors were amazing. Most breakfasts are served with a side of potato wedges, refried beans, and soft steamy flour tortillas, tasty ways to neutralize the flavor fiesta in your mouth.

Those in your party feeling less adventurous won't be left out at this restaurant. Along with these medleys of Mexican dishes, breakfasters might also choose pancakes, fruit, or cereal.

Recommended reading: New Mexico's Trail of the Painted Ponies began as a public art project in 2000. To date, 155 ponies have been created. Look for life sized painted ponies as you travel around the Land of Enchantment, or find a great book that documents the horse artwork. The Trail of Painted Ponies by the New Mexico Public Art Project and HorsePower New Mexico is a colorful review of this project.

Meridian Espresso & News

228 Old Santa Fe Trail
(505) 989-9252

Breakfast Hours:
Monday-Friday 7am-6pm,
Saturday-Sunday 7am-7pm
Kid Component: *
Parking: Street and municipal lots
Area: Plaza
Prices: $

Headlines at Meridian Espresso & News:

Breakfast choices: burritos, sandwiches, bagels, and a wide array of pastry items. Sold until they run out, usually by noon or 1:00 p.m.

Sign on the counter: "Bicycle Commuters! Ride your bike to Meridian and get 20% off your daily coffee drink!"

Sign on the door: "We are looking for a good barista. Interested? Inquire within."

Message on the Customer Suggestion Forms: "Comments? Suggestions? Ideas? We wanna know! Put 'em down here and stick 'em in the box! Thanks!"

Newsbriefs:

Many of the customer suggestions are tacked to the wall in the "Condiments" area, and at least half feature cartoons, sketches, and doodles, from rudimentary to manga-esque sophistication. Our favorite comment was "Elvis is in the building! He's sitting in that black leather chair nearest the cash register! Check it out!" A perhaps more realistic remark quipped, "Great place to surf and the food is excellent!" The short and sweet said "Awesome yum-yums!" And the illustrated question asked, "What would Jesus drink?"

Unfortunately, we missed Elvis. But we have seen that particular chair occupied by a fellow sipping coffee and working on his laptop. Maybe he was trying to contact The King via e-mail, thanks to Meridian's free high-speed wireless Internet.

Speaking of mail, Meridian sells a line of postcards that might seem too funky at first glance. But after sipping your beverage and nibbling a brownie or other goodie, you just might think of the perfect friend or relative for one of the cards. Mailing is a cinch, thanks to the convenient cluster of mailboxes on the patio near the front entrance.

Hot drinks include espresso, macchiato, cappuccino, latte, mocha, Americano, tea, chai, and Mexican cocoa, and can be served iced on request. Cold drinks include frappés, lemonade, sodas, juices, and smoothies.

When admiring the décor, which includes a very fine wood counter and matching serving areas, look up and marvel at the shiny ceiling. There's also a bulletin board in the corner of the eating area covered with flyers and announcements about interesting upcoming events.

The round umbrella-topped tables outside feature traditional ice-cream parlor chairs, with wire backs twisted into heart shapes.

Recommended reading: The classic childhood tale of Little Red Riding Hood gets a southwestern makeover in Isabel and the Hungry Coyote/Isabel y el coyote hambriento *by Keith Polette. If only the hungry coyote had dropped by Meridian for some of those "awesome yum-yums" instead of trying to talk Isabel out of the goodies in her basket!*

Museum Hill Café

Camino Lejo, on Museum Hill
(505) 473-9600

*www.walterburkecatering.com/
index.asp*

Breakfast hours:
Sundays 11am-3pm
Kid Component: *
Parking: Plentiful
Area: Midtown
Prices: $$$

Don't be fooled. The Museum Hill Café is not just for tourists and people visiting some of Santa Fe's finest museums. The Museum Hill Café should be a destination eating locale for Santa Fe residents and visitors alike. If you are a Sunday Museum Hill visitor, plan time for a leisurely brunch between exploring exhibits at the Museum of International Folk Art and the Museum of Indian Arts and Culture. If you have already seen the museum exhibits, make a Sunday trip up the hill to the café that boasts its Sunday best as: "Brunch with a View."

Museum Hill has some of the most stunning views in town. To the west lie the Jemez Mountains. There are four to five lucky tables along the westward facing windows. Fortunately, all the windows in the café are gigantic, and the beautiful distant landscape can be seen from almost every table.

The café is modern with lots of dark woods. The walls inside are decorated with Native American weavings and sculptures. All the art in the restaurant is for sale. Outdoor dining is available in only the very warmest weather.

The menu at the café changes seasonally. You won't always find Santa Fe's beloved breakfast burrito on the menu, but you won't miss it. Entrées at Museum Hill are treasured gourmet works of art that can be savored amidst the hum of café conversation and the view of New Mexico's ever changing, always stunning skies.

Our breakfast burrito-loving friend gladly traded his normal breakfast fare for the huevos rancheros. The huevos are served atop corn

tortillas and smothered in Chimayó red chile. All of this is topped with cheese and served with rice and black beans.

We also loved the eggs Benedict served with ham and tomatoes. This perfectly prepared breakfast comes with mixed salad greens topped with balsamic vinaigrette. The hollandaise sauce and the vinaigrette complemented each other perfectly.

Freshly squeezed orange juice, teas, espressos, cappuccinos, and lattes are among the wide assortment of beverage options. Mimosas are available after noon on Sundays.

The entrées are a treat in themselves, and are not overly filling. We could have made it through the rest of the day without another bite of food, but decided instead to take the waitress up on her dessert suggestion. We indulged in the bread pudding, a 4-inch square slice of cranberry and piñon bread topped with a steaming hot sugar sauce. It was rich and filling, and allowed us fifteen more minutes to enjoy the view of a storm moving quickly over the Jemez Mountains. Brunch with this view is the perfect start to a Sunday filled with family, friends, and culture.

Recommended reading: If your plans include a visit to the Museum of Indian Arts and Culture, be sure to check out the Museum of New Mexico's I Am Here: Two Thousand Years of Southwest Indian Arts and Culture *by Andrew Hunter Whiteford and Stewart Peckham.*

New York Deli

4056 Cerrillos Road
(505) 424-1200

Breakfast hours:
Daily 7am-3pm
Kid Component: **
Parking: Plentiful
Area: Cerrillos
Prices: $$

The New York Deli is on the corner of Cerrillos and Rodeo Road, a perfect location for folks heading into town from the south end of Santa Fe, or for commuters driving up from Albuquerque for a long day at the office. Especially for this clientele, the New York Deli has a "commuter special" on its menu available from 7:00 a.m. to 9:00 a.m. (your choice of bagel topped with plain cream cheese and a large coffee to go for less than three dollars). The New York Deli, however, is more than just breakfast on the run.

If you left home without a newspaper, take a look at the newspaper boxes outside the restaurant and consider purchasing the *New York Times*, the *Wall Street Journal*, *USA Today*, the *Santa Fe New Mexican*, or the *Journal Santa Fe*. If you are short on coins, the weekly *Santa Fe Reporter* can be picked up for free.

Despite the "wait to be seated signs," early breakfast eaters should order breakfast at the counter and have a seat in the café section of the restaurant. The restaurant is a basic deli with café tables and chairs. You can help yourself to juice and sodas in the refrigerators and prepare your own coffee or tea. The restaurant walls are decorated with giant historic photographs of New York City, movie posters, and 8x10 glossies of movie stars. In warmer seasons, dining outside in front of the deli is ideal.

There is a large selection of sit-down made-to-order breakfast specialties including moons over my hammy (a toasted English muffin topped with ham, two eggs, melted cheddar cheese all served with home fries) and steak Philly and eggs (thinly sliced steak grilled with

peppers, onions, and Monterey jack cheese all topped with two eggs and served with home fries and a bagel of your choice). The menu also includes pancake, French toast and cereal options. Vegetarian diners will find a lot of options including the tofu scrambler (scrambled eggs with grilled marinated tofu, mushrooms, tomatoes, and onions served with home fries and a bagel).

We can highly recommend the Brooklyn breakfast burrito, a burrito that is slightly different from the usual chile-drenched breakfast burritos found in Santa Fe. The entrée is a flour tortilla wrapped around scrambled eggs and potatoes, and is topped with cheddar cheese and green chile. The cheese is more plentiful than the green chile, which we found as a welcome change. We also really enjoyed the potato pancakes (potato rounds perfectly flavored with a significant touch of onion, and served with a bowl of sour cream and a bowl of applesauce).

We loved the standard house coffee. Specialty morning coffees, teas, and espresso drinks are also available.

Bagels are the biggest menu item at the New York Deli. While standing in line to place your order, a neon sign proclaims "hot bagels." The bagel variety is supreme. Choices include freshly made poppy seed, cinnamon raisin, green chile, vegetable, blueberry and sun dried tomato bagels just to name a few. Cream cheese toppings include "verry" berry, green chile, honey walnut, and a variety of lite cream cheese choices. Bagels are always generously topped with your selected spread.

Recommended reading: The Santa Fe Reporter *is one of the free papers you can pick up outside the New York Deli. Also pick up Richard McCord's book,* The Other State: New Mexico, USA. *McCord and his wife, Laurie Knowles, founded the* Santa Fe Reporter *in the early 1970s after they moved to Santa Fe from New York City. The book chronicles some of McCord's most interesting early experiences in Santa Fe.*

Over Easy Café

2801 Rodeo Road
(505) 474-6336

Breakfast Hours:
Tuesday-Friday 6:30am-2pm,
Saturday-Sunday 7am-2pm
Kid Component: **
Parking: Plentiful
Area: Midtown
Prices: $$

Looking for a new favorite place to eat every weekend? Our recommendation is the Over Easy Café. Along with amazing food, the people behind the counter at the Over Easy are some of the friendliest people you will encounter in Santa Fe. If you find yourself frequenting this eatery, you will be called by name as you walk through the front door on your way to your first meal of the day.

The mission printed on the Over Easy's menu states, "We strive to serve the finest New Mexican dishes in a fast family friendly atmosphere." After numerous experiences at this restaurant, we can confidently report that the café's mission has been accomplished. The restaurant serves breakfast almost as fast as a fast-food restaurant, but the food is remarkably superior. Families with children are welcome, but adult diners eating alone will also find the restaurant quite comfortable. And friendly. If you thought you were a bit short on friends when you walked in the door, as you leave the Over Easy Café, you may feel like you have picked up a new friend or two.

The restaurant is filled with small café chairs and tables for 2-4 people. In warmer weather, outside seating is available. Whether eating on a weekday or weekend, the restaurant is buzzing with activity, but you will never find yourself waiting long for your order.

Diners can easily order take-out or eat-in at the counter. If you decide to eat in, your food will be brought to your table, and you will feel well taken care of by the Over Easy owner and staff.

There is a large selection of healthy breakfast options, including the largest low-carb breakfast menu in town. Low-carb options include a

five carb breakfast burrito, six carb French toast, nine carb pancakes, and a six carb huevos rancheros plate.

Ordering from the regular breakfast carb-filled menu, we loved the tortilla hash, a breakfast version of frito pie. In this dish, eggs, chorizo, potatoes, cheese, and chile top strips of corn tortilla chips. We also really enjoyed the breakfast burrito. The burritos are served smothered for dine-in customers, and are available in a handheld version for breakfasters on the run.

For chile-sensitive diners, checkout the "chile rating" posted on the board under the menu. On our visits, we found the green chile relatively mild and quite flavorful. If chile isn't an option in your breakfast repertoire, try the pancakes or French toast. Weekend sweet eaters will be pleased to find the Saturday and Sunday special, apple pannekoeken. The Over Easy Café's version of this morning treat is made up of juicy sliced apples embedded in a thick cinnamon cake. The pancake is as large as the dinner plate on which it is served, and the dish is topped with a nice layer of powdered sugar. A great way to start the weekend.

The Over Easy Café is located in Rodeo Plaza, where Rodeo Road and Zia Road meet. See you there!

Recommended reading: University of New Mexico Librarian Claire Reynier visits Santa Fe numerous times when she learns that one of her college friends has been murdered in her fashionable Santa Fe home. To solve this mystery, pick up Judith Van Gieson's Confidence Woman.

Pancakes on the Plaza

Breakfast Hours:
July 4th, 7am-noon (or when they run out of food!)
Kid Component: ***
Parking: Since it's a holiday, parking is free at parking meters!
Area: Plaza
Prices: $

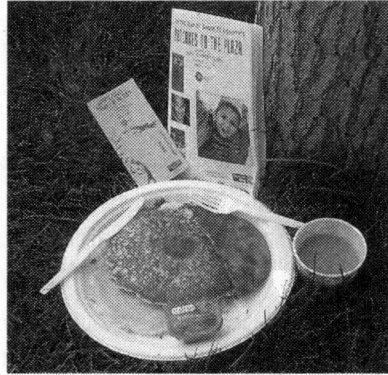

We've talked about places where breakfast is available seven days a week, and served all day. We've described restaurants that only dispense this important meal during certain hours. We've mentioned locations that do breakfast just two days a week, or even only on Sunday.

Now we're going to rave about a breakfast that's served once a year!

If you happen to be in Santa Fe on the 4th of July, and are in the mood for flapjacks, step right up. It's "Pancakes on the Plaza!"

For 30 years, this event that puts the fun in fundraising has been benefitting programs of the local United Way of Santa Fe County. Tickets can be purchased on site, or at a modest savings in advance.

The menu is simple: pancakes, ham or vegetarian sausage, butter and syrup, coffee, orange juice, and milk. Even though you might have to wait for a few minutes in an enormous line, the lines moves swiftly and the service is streamlined. Multiple serving setups provide plenty of opportunities for you to pick up your plate of hotcakes. There are rows and rows of tables and benches set up on Lincoln Avenue between the Plaza bandstand and the portal of the Palace of the Governors. There are also chairs in front of the bandstand, and the usual array of Plaza benches. If you enjoy the unpredictability of having your plate in your lap, stake out a patch of grass, preferably under a tree.

Serving begins at 7:00 a.m. and so does the entertainment. If you're

an early bird, you might hear the Star Spangled Banner played live by the Santa Fe Concert Band, made more special by the sound of the crowd singing along.

After we ate and enjoyed the entertainment for awhile, we stood at the end of one of the long tents and observed the pancake production line.

We also ventured over to the annual car show along Lincoln Avenue, where polished antique cars line the curbs, children ride on their dads' shoulders holding patriotic pinwheels, and dogs walk proudly with their car-admiring owners. The car show is not only a great opportunity to see beautiful classic cars, but it also offers the chance to talk to some of these automobile enthusiasts about the unique history and events that have touched their vehicles.

Several arts and craft vendors line the side streets around the Plaza. If you didn't get your fill of pancakes, a food vendor will gladly sell you an ear of roasted corn or a hotdog on a stick.

Pancakes on the Plaza, a very mellow occasion attended by hundreds of Santa Fe residents and visitors, is much more laid back than other internationally recognized events that take place on the Plaza in the summer. Red, white, and blue clothing is in evidence, along with plenty of wild headgear.

If you want to see real Santa Feans enjoying the very heart of their city on Independence Day, you'll flip for Pancakes on the Plaza!

Recommended reading: Most of the action in Barbara Beasley Murphy's Miguel Lost & Found in the Palace *takes place inside the Palace of the Governors. The book is the first in the* Museo Kids *series.*

Pantry Restaurant

1820 Cerrillos Road
(505) 986-0022

www.santafestation.com/pantry/
index.html

Breakfast Hours:
Monday-Saturday 6:30am-9:00pm,
Sunday 7am-9:00pm
Kid Component: ***
Parking: Plentiful
Area: Cerrillos
Prices: $$

The Pantry Restaurant is a long-time favorite of Santa Feans and a wonderful casual dining option for visitors who want to have a real local breakfast experience. As a testament to its popularity, a sign behind the register reports that the restaurant uses two tons of potatoes, 16,200 eggs, and 493 pounds of fresh coffee every month.

There are distinct dining areas in the restaurant. If you are dining alone or in need of a quick bite, stake out a stool at the counter and watch wait staff pick up the food that pours out of the kitchen. The front room of the Pantry has café tables. The best seat in the house is a table-for-two in front of the building's main window, affording a clear view of the busy traffic on Cerrillos Road. Most of the seating is in the back room, where you will find a giant mural on the south wall artfully depicting New Mexico's history and geography. If you have children dining with you, you will probably feel most comfortable in this spacious room.

No matter where you sit, this restaurant is known for its great breakfasts. Our favorite entrée is the breakfast burrito with bacon and red or green chile. Most breakfasts are served with perfectly seasoned red chile potatoes (Pantry fries) and pinto beans. A smaller version of the burrito is the breakfast sandwich with the same ingredients as the breakfast burrito, but in a single fold of a tortilla. Yet another spicy breakfast specialty is huevos consuelo (eggs on a corn tortilla smothered with a tasty sauce). The sweet breakfasts are

also recommended. The stuffed pancakes are folded and filled with fresh mouthwatering blueberries or strawberries. The Belgian waffle is also a favorite. Both sweet breakfasts include real whipped cream that perfectly balances the fruit.

If you find yourself at the Pantry on a weekend morning, be prepared for a wait. There is plenty of outdoor seating where you can watch cars and pedestrians on Santa Fe's main thoroughfare, but be sure to bundle up if visiting during the winter months. Eating at the Pantry is always worth the wait. We have dined here nearly 30 times in the last four years and consistently find great service and wonderful food.

Before leaving, be sure to take a close look at the framed movie poster, Heart of the Golden West, featuring Roy Rogers and Trigger that hangs on the wall by the end of the lunch counter. Also admire the quilt over the fireplace that depicts the restaurant. If you've been dining with children, you'll recognize the design. It appears on the placemat that the youngsters received (along with crayons) when they were seated.

Recommended reading: In her book, Only in Santa Fe, *Denise Kusel writes, "When I wrote my first check for $2.56 for a breakfast in a place most people spoke Spanglish and the chile was hot enough to spring new tears into my eyes, I knew I had arrived in a place that mattered."*

Plaza Bakery

56 East San Francisco Street (corner
of East San Francisco Street and
Lincoln Ave)
(505) 988-3858

Breakfast Hours:
Daily 7 am-closing, (9 or 10pm
depending on business)
Kid Component: *
Parking: Street and municipal lots
Area: Plaza
Prices: $

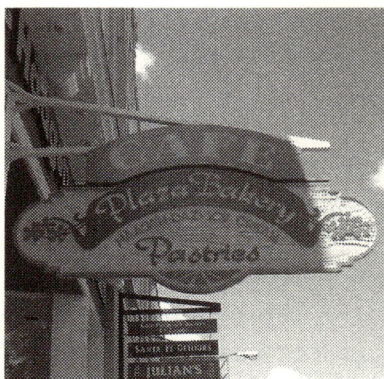

Eating solo? Looking for the best people-watching location in Santa
Fe? Head for the Plaza Bakery on the corner of East San Francisco
Street and Lincoln Avenue. Place your order and then settle into one
of two seats at the countertop table built into the window facing
the street. Early in the morning you'll witness the non-stop parade
of delivery trucks traveling up San Francisco after dropping off their
loads. We've seen the same UPS man on several occasions. He always
has to park on the sidewalk to avoid blocking traffic completely.
We've also observed Santa Feans heading toward their offices or
places of business in the Plaza area. Probably more women wearing
fancy concho belts walk by this corner than any other place in town.
Locals and tourists alike pass by later in the morning when stores
are open. Jewelry sellers sit off in the distance under the portal at
the Palace of the Governors. All along the block are the strollers on
Lincoln Avenue. By strollers we mean people strolling, but you'll also
see babies and toddlers in strollers, individuals with dogs on leashes,
and maybe . . . no fooling! . . . a dog in a stroller! The day we saw
the dog riding in the stroller we vowed that our next book should be
Pets Santa Fe Style.

No matter what time of day you're here, you might get so absorbed in
looking out the window that you forget to eat. Don't let that happen!
Specific breakfast dishes and lunch specialties are served anytime, so
your choices here are extensive. If you're in a breakfast food frame of
mind, look at the breakfast pastries: croissants, Danishes, turnovers,
muffins, bagels, and breads. For something more substantial, we

recommend the ham and potato quiche (a generous slice, not just a sliver!). "Good Morning Santa Fe" is toasted French bread, eggs, ham and Swiss cheese. There are meat or veggie burritos, the frittata (a veggie baked omelet), and a fruit bowl that includes a scoop of sorbet.

Did we say sorbet? The Plaza Bakery is also your source for Haagen-Dazs ice cream – lots of flavors, lots of possibilities. It's never too early for ice cream!

We were tempted to try some of the lunch specialties for breakfast, particularly the spanokopita: spinach, feta cheese, and kalamata olives in a pastry crust. But if a potato veggie knish, quesadilla, stuffed croissant, or spicy chicken wrap is calling your name, give in!

Speaking of calling . . . we noticed that nearly half of the passersby seemed to be talking on cell phones. Many were chatting on the move, but others just stood on the corner and yakked. What are they talking about? Maybe they're spreading the word about the dog in the stroller!

Recommended reading: While standing in the Plaza, Josh, Steenie, and Marcia have a detailed food discussion during Las Fiestas del Corazón Sagrado in Richard Bradford's classic coming-of-age novel set in New Mexico: Red Sky at Morning.

Plaza Café South Side

3011 Cerrillos Rd
(505) 424-0755

*www.999dine.com/nm/
southsidecafe/*

Breakfast Hours:
Daily full breakfast menu 7am-11am,
smaller breakfast menu 11am-9pm
Kid Component: ***
Parking: Plentiful

Area: Cerrillos
Prices: $$

To set the scene, in 1970 the city of Santa Fe had a population of 41,167 residents. In 1975 Santa Fe had a volunteer fire department, 37 churches, 5 banks, and 5 savings and loans. In the mid 1970s, no neon lights were allowed in the city and no commercial airplanes flew to Santa Fe. With all this in mind, you can step back into the 1970s when you enter the Plaza Café South Side, the fabulous restaurant attached to the Quality Inn on Cerrillos Road.

The Plaza Café South Side is a newly remodeled restaurant decorated in a funky 1970s style with eight large, comfortable, blue vinyl window booths and six tables with maroon vinyl chairs through the middle of the restaurant. If you are dining alone or waiting for a to-go order, enjoy the restaurant from one of the lunch counter chairs where you can watch the cooks in the kitchen.

The Plaza Café South Side is the sister of the Plaza Restaurant on Santa Fe's downtown Plaza. The restaurants have similar menus, but the South Side location offers delicious and fascinating cuisine without the burden of having to hunt for downtown parking or navigate the swarms of people visiting the Plaza.

The South Side serves generous breakfast menu options until 11:00 a.m. Choices include huevos rancheros served with beans, hash browns, and soft flour tortillas; blue corn enchiladas (a corn tortilla topped with eggs, chipotle, and tomatillo salsas, guacamole, and sour cream); and the chile relleno omelet (breaded beef steak and two eggs topped with chile and cheese). Bakery goods include muffins and cinnamon rolls.

The extensive menu at the Plaza Café South Side has made this restaurant one of our favorite haunts. We love the huevos divorciados (scrambled eggs rolled in a flour tortilla). Half of the dish is topped with red chile and cheese and the other half is topped with green chile and cheese. Since we can't decide if we like the red or green chile at South Side better, we were happy to find the huevos divorsidaos, so we don't have to choose! The breakfast burrito is also a traditional favorite.

We have devoured several breakfast sandwiches during our breakfast research. The South Side grilled ham and egg sandwich comes on bread slicked with Dijon mustard, asadero cheese, ham, and green chile. Most outstanding, however, is the grilled chocolate sandwich (challah bread spread with chocolate ganache, grilled, and dusted with powdered sugar). This is good. Have we ever lied to you? You can trust us. We're librarians!

Recommended reading: After visiting the Plaza Café South Side, you might wonder what life in Santa Fe was like in the 1970s. Jean and John Cartwright's 1976, Enjoy Santa Fe More, *is a fun peek into Santa Fe's recent past.*

Plaza Restaurant

54 Lincoln Avenue
(505) 982-1664

Breakfast Hours:
Daily 7am-11am
Kid Component: **
Parking: Street and municipal lots
Area: Plaza
Prices: $$

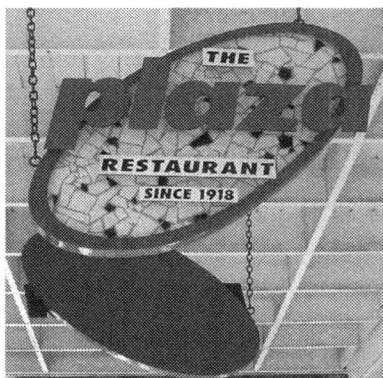

Standing in the middle of Santa Fe's downtown Plaza, it is possible to turn in a circle and get a feel for Santa Fe's rich history. The Palace of the Governors on the Plaza's north side was originally constructed by the Spanish government in the early 1600s. It now serves as the State of New Mexico's history museum. Native Americans sit under the Palace's portal and sell jewelry. The Plaza has witnessed war and celebration. It was the center of the city's economy at the end of the Santa Fe Trail, and continues to serve as the heart of Santa Fe's tourist economy. But this isn't a history or economics book, this is a book about Santa Fe's breakfasts!

On the west side, you will find one of the few places on the Plaza that serves breakfast, the Plaza Restaurant. In the cold and bitter winter months, patrons will walk through the front door and then push away a heavy cloth (as if entering a busy theater stage) to come into the restaurant. This traditional diner is decorated with tiny white tiles and a beautiful white tin ceiling. The restaurant has some booth seating and a banquette around the wall, so mixed seating is available (banquette and café chairs at the same table). The heavy wood dining room chairs are well worn, well loved, and if they could talk, would probably have some very interesting stories to share. If you are fortunate enough to get seated near the front of the restaurant, you will have a nice view of early morning Plaza activities.

The diner also has a lunch counter where you can sit and watch the wait staff prepare morning drinks. The wall above the lunch counter is tiled with broken black and white plates. The back wall displays a large map of New Mexico outlined in neon. Other interesting wall

decorations include a Viven las Fiestas poster featuring Zozobra, and boards that list important phone numbers for the mayor, the governor, state senators and representatives, plus the chief of police, and the daily weather forecast.

In tourist destinations across the country, restaurants can capitalize on their great location yet provide poor food or service. The Plaza Restaurant will not disappoint tourists or locals in any of these ways. It has a friendly wait staff and cooks that dream up fantastic breakfasts. The huge breakfast menu includes tasty harvest oatmeal with fruit, granola, and yogurt; baked from scratch cinnamon rolls; blue corn piñon hotcakes; and the chile relleno omelet (green chile stuffed with cheese and cooked into a three egg omelet). We recommend all of these items as well as the lovingly made carnitas (pork cooked with onions and green chile served with eggs any way you like them and pinto beans). The Plaza Restaurant offers a very hearty breakfast to begin a day filled with visiting downtown museums, bookstores, churches, and shops.

The morning drinks at the Plaza Restaurant are also well prepared and will make your taste buds sing. Freshly squeezed orange juice, apple juice, grapefruit juice, and lemonade are available. Espresso drinks are also on the menu. Our favorite drink here is the iced chai latte. You won't find a better drink for breakfast near the Plaza.

Recommended reading: All of Santa Fe's walking tours take visitors to the Plaza. For a virtual walk through Santa Fe's historic downtown, pick up a copy of Kingsley Hammett's Santa Fe: A Walk through Time. *Detective Joshua Croft stops by the Plaza Restaurant for a bowl of green chile stew in* At Ease with the Dead *by Santa Fe author Walter Satterthwait.*

Posa's
El Merendero

3538 Zafarano Drive
(505) 473-3454

1514 Rodeo Road
(505) 471-4766

www.santafetamales.com

Breakfast Hours:
Monday-Saturday 8am-11:30am,
Sunday 10am-12:30pm
Kid Component: **

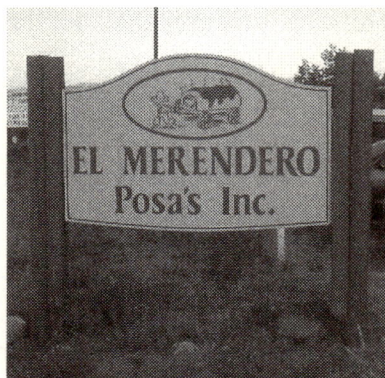

Parking: Plentiful
Area: Cerrillos & Midtown
Prices: $

Posa's El Merendero has two locations in Santa Fe and both offer casual dining and take out service. Eating in, diners will find sparsely decorated dining rooms with red and white tabletops. Step up to the counter and place your order from the overhead menu. Diners serve themselves beverages including sodas, coffee, and tea. For a special morning treat, add a squeeze of fresh lime to your beverage of choice. Limes are available at the drink preparation station.

We have spent years enjoying Santa Fe's great breakfast offerings, and have tried breakfast burritos at just about every restaurant in town. This small unassuming restaurant nearly tops our "Santa Fe's Best Breakfast Burrito" list. Yet, Posa's is not really known for its superior burritos at breakfast. The restaurant's claim to fame is tamales. According to the menu, tamales can be ordered online at http://www.santafetamales.com.

We have to agree, Posa's tamales are out of this world. The tamales come with red chile and pork, green chile with chicken, green chile with cheese, and green chile with vegetables. So before heading out of town on your way to explore Taos or Las Vegas, grab a bag of tamales (remember the forks and lots of napkins) and head to a picnic area to partake in this glorious food.

Back to the amazing breakfast burritos. Burritos are available with bacon, sausage, chorizo, and/or potato. Posa's does a lot of take out business, and these burritos can be made quickly for your breakfast

on the run. For a little more money, all of the burritos are available in a smothered version (topped with cheese and red or green chile). Handheld burritos are served wrapped in white paper, and smothered burritos come in a Styrofoam box. These burritos are so great, it is a shame they aren't served on china or, at the very least, on Fiestaware, These breakfast delights should be savored in elegance.

The burritos are thick and juicy. If you take your food on the go from Posa's, be sure to order a large drink, grab at least five napkins to wipe the sweat from your brow, and take 10 additional napkins to clean your hands and face. These burritos are so amazing, they are worth the mess!

Recommended reading: Tamales are definitely comfort food. The Tamale Quilt, by Jane Tenorio-Coscarelli, features a story, a recipe, and a quilt pattern.

Rio Chama Steakhouse

414 Old Santa Fe Trail
(505) 955-0765

www.riochamasteakhouse.com

Breakfast Hours:
Saturday-Sunday 10am-2:30pm
Kid Component: **
Parking: Limited parking behind the
restaurant, street and municipal lots

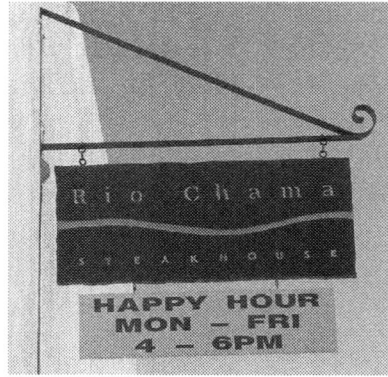

Area: Plaza
Prices: $$$

Have you ever wanted to share a meal with New Mexico's governor? Have you ever needed to casually run into a state senator? Have you ever had the desire to sit at a bar with a Hollywood actress? If the answer to any of these questions is "yes," then you might want to frequent the Rio Chama Steakhouse, an elegant restaurant less than a block from New Mexico's capitol building.

The Rio Chama is largely known for its award-wining bar and tender steaks. Weekend brunches at Rio Chama are outstanding and are, sadly, not well known. Brunch is served on Saturdays and Sundays, and while Santa Fe's rich and famous residents might not venture to the Rio Chama Steakhouse for breakfast, you will feel both rich and famous as you luxuriate in this beautiful restaurant. The highly skilled servers at this dining establishment are at your beck and call, and the professional chefs will create gourmet masterpieces that will never disappoint your taste buds. Heavy polished silverware adorns the dark wood tables. Waiters drop thick white cloth napkins into your lap and bring your drinks to you on a silver tray.

The Rio Chama has a comfortable southwest sophistication without the stuffy feeling of some of Santa Fe's high-end restaurants. While we almost always recommend outdoor seating in Santa Fe, this adobe-walled restaurant has amazing indoor and outdoor seating. Inside, red carpets and wooden floors run beneath your feet, and tin chandeliers and wall sconces elegantly light the small rooms. Outside, brick patios, outdoor fireplaces, and padded iron furniture will delightfully comfort you.

Steak should be a breakfast option at any good steakhouse, and the Rio Chama is no exception. The steak and eggs entrée comes with steak asada and eggs cooked to your liking. Breakfast potatoes are an outstanding tasty side dish, mixed with sautéed onions, red pepper, and green pepper. Another favorite breakfast is the ham and eggs. This entrée comes with a thick slice of smoked ham, eggs cooked to order, breakfast potatoes, and raisin toast. The raisin toast alone was a wonderful breakfast treat. The soft bread came with a raisin and a nut in every bite. We also highly recommend the breakfast burrito, a traditional breakfast burrito seasoned with onions and tomatoes all topped with cheddar cheese and red or green chile. The burrito comes with a side of pinto beans.

Sweet tooth diners are not left out at the Rio Chama. Belgian waffles, blueberry flapjacks, and French toast stuffed with cream cheese are also on the menu.

Alcoholic beverages are available for breakfast and are highly recommended. The fruity sangria was a refreshing complement to our meaty meals. Also try a morning mimosa or Bloody Mary.

Recommended reading: Enrique Garcia runs for governor (and may even eat at the Rio Chama Steakhouse) in Norman Zollinger's The Road to Santa Fe.

Santa Fe Baking Company Café

504 West Cordova Road
(505) 988-4292

Breakfast Hours:
Daily 6am-8pm
Kid Component: *
Parking: Plentiful
Area: Midtown
Prices: $$

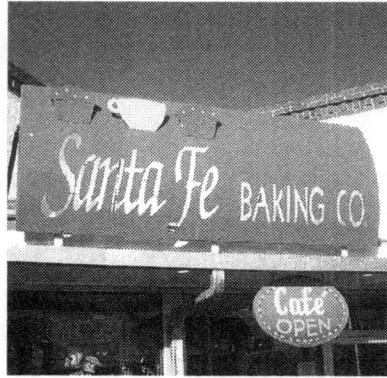

Whether you visit the Santa Fe Baking Company Café on a weekday or weekend, you will find this to be Santa Fe's busiest and most entertaining coffee house. And if that isn't enough, breakfast is served all day! This café is located in the strip mall on the corner of St. Francis Drive and Cordova Road and is busy on weekday mornings and packed on weekends. Dogs are welcome in the outside dining area, and the restaurant has free wireless Internet access for patrons with laptops. By 8:00 a.m. every day, the place is buzzing with business people, artists, college students, and retired community members.

The Santa Fe Baking Company Café is actually much more than a coffee house. Along with a wide range of coffees (four house coffees served daily), teas, and espresso drinks, the restaurant bakes an amazing assortment of pastries, has a large variety of sit-down meals, and includes a full juice bar with an almost infinite number of smoothie options.

There is a near constant rush of people coming to the restaurant for coffee and pastries to go. Those diners wanting to sit down and enjoy a more leisurely start to the day will find the restaurant is largely filled with Santa Fe locals and people who live within walking distance of the café. Café tables are huge and allow plenty of room for food, newspapers, and laptop computing.

On weekday mornings from 8:00 a.m. to 9:00 a.m. Santa Fe's public radio, KSFR 90.7, broadcasts "Radio Café" from a corner table in the restaurant. The broadcast is a low-key affair, and unless you are watching carefully, the radio show may start and finish without any notice.

If you are dining here for the first time, there is a system for ordering food. As you come in the front door you will see bright yellow menus with an enormous variety of food options. Take your menu and stand in the line leading toward the cash register. Menu options include French, Greek and Santa Fe omelets; steak and eggs; waffles; pancakes; fruit; homemade granola; bagels; muffins; and breakfast burritos. Vegetarian options are denoted with a petroglyph-styled turtle. At the register you will place your order, and if you have ordered an entrée you will give your name. When your entrée is ready, a waiter will wander around the restaurant calling your name until he finds you.

We really enjoyed our breakfasts at this café. Along with watching people, we highly recommend the cowboy bowl. This brimming blend of black beans, fried potatoes, cheddar cheese, tomatoes, green chile sauce, and scallions is topped with one egg any style and a dollop of sour cream, accompanied by a warm flour tortilla. Obviously designed for a hungry cowboy, this flavorful feast in a bowl will hold you for a full day of cow punching or other activities. We also truly enjoy the AM sandwich: eggs and cheddar cheese between bagel or herb biscuit halves (we recommend the biscuit). Topping options for the AM sandwich include ham and tomatoes, both great additions to this amazing meal.

Recommended reading: If you enjoy listening to local talk-radio like the "Radio Café," you will enjoy reading The Best of From the Plaza *edited by William Baxter and Matt Kelly. The chapters in this book are radio interviews with Santa Fe locals about some of the city's historic folklore.*

Santa Fe Bar & Grill

187 Paseo de Peralta, in
De Vargas Mall
(505) 982-3033

www.santafebargrill.com/

Breakfast Hours:
Sunday 11am-3pm
Kid Component: ***
Parking: Plentiful
Area: Midtown
Prices: $$

Sleeping in on Sunday mornings is one of the greatest things about the weekend. As you wake up and begin to formulate your late start, grab the large Sunday edition of the *Santa Fe New Mexican*, and head for the Santa Fe Bar and Grill at the De Vargas Mall. The restaurant serves breakfast/brunch only on Sundays.

The Santa Fe Bar and Grill feels like a contemporary big city restaurant. It has touches of Santa Fe style, but it is, by and large, a dimly lit bustling modern establishment. If you wish to eat inside, you will be seated at a café table. About half of the tables have one banco/booth seat and one chair. So if the question "do you want a booth or a table?" is a source of stress on a Sunday morning, you do not have to choose. You also may opt to sit on a high stool at the large wooden bar.

For most of the year you will have the option of sitting outside on the mostly shaded brick patio. The patio has rather comfortable metal furniture with potted plants on every table. It overlooks the De Vargas Mall parking lot, which is fairly quiet on Sunday mornings. If you are dining with children, the patio is ideal, and children get crayons and a picture to color while waiting for breakfast.

With your giant Sunday newspaper in hand, take a seat and examine the brunch menu before scanning the real estate section for promising open houses. The menu holds something for everyone, including huevos rancheros, French toast, fish tacos, and grilled cheese

sandwiches. If you arrive after noon, you will also have the option of ordering a mimosa, tequila Maria, or a Bloody Mary from the bar. If you arrive before noon, or don't have a taste for an alcoholic beverage with breakfast, you won't be disappointed. The Santa Fe Bar and Grill also has specialty brunch drinks including freshly squeezed orange juice and strawberry or raspberry liquados, which are thick fresh tasting fruit smoothies.

We highly recommend the quiche and salad. The salad greens come topped with small carrots, green peppers, and sweet jicama. We love the house dressing with this salad, and the quiche is always good. On our recent visits, the quiche has been filled with ham, onions, cheddar cheese, and green chile. A perfect meal. You can't go wrong with the breakfast burrito, either. Burritos come with the option for guacamole and arrive with a side of barbeque beans and potatoes. A frequent companion invariably orders the grilled cheese and tomato sandwich (jack, cheddar, or Swiss cheese on black bread or organic white with mayonnaise, served with house basil pesto). It's served with a choice of house fries, fresh potato chips, or coleslaw, and bacon can be included for an additional charge. The entrées at Santa Fe Bar and Grill are served on steel plates, and the wait staff won't let you sit with an empty glass.

Recommended reading: If visiting Santa Fe's Sunday open houses is one of your hobbies, you will also enjoy The Small Adobe House *by Agnesa Reeve and Robert Reck.*

St. Francis Hotel – The Club

210 Don Gaspar
(505) 983-5700

*www.hotelstfrancis.com/
dining_club.php*

Breakfast Hours:
Daily 7am-2pm
Kid Component: **
Parking: For hotel guests, street and
municipal lots

Area: Plaza
Prices: $$

Just walking into the St. Francis Hotel you feel important. The huge doors to the hotel open into a large tiled lobby. Hotel employees await your arrival at the old wooden reservation desk. Roomy couches and chairs sit mostly vacant in front of the fireplace just waiting for your tired body after an energetic stroll through Santa Fe's oldest neighborhoods and narrowest streets. But it is breakfast time, and you are looking for The Club.

Upon entering the hotel lobby from Don Gaspar, head toward the reservation desk, turn right at the desk and follow the short hallway back to the hostess's podium. She may ask, "Would you prefer to sit inside or out on the patio?" At this juncture you have a tough decision. The Club has one of the best sightseeing dining rooms in town. If you choose inside, ask to sit near one of the giant picture windows where you will be able to watch people walk up and down Don Gaspar and Water Streets. You may see the jaywalking woman with big blonde hair, spiky black heels, and oversized turquoise jewelry *really* is carrying a white miniature poodle in her handbag and the dog *really* does have pink-painted claws. You may also notice that the man sitting across the street wearing a cowboy hat and a leather shirt has a parrot on his shoulder and *really* is wearing a skirt, and it suits him well!

No one would fault you for leaving this menagerie behind for the option of sitting on the patio on a clear cool New Mexico morning. The walled brick patio has about ten outdoor tables with protective green umbrellas. The outdoor seating is quiet and sheltered, but does

have wooden doors that open on to Water Street allowing occasional glimpses of street activity. The patio is a peaceful place to eat outside, and is a mere block away from Santa Fe's Plaza. Potted flowers and a stone fountain add a calming atmosphere.

The breakfast menu has daily specials ranging from an early week eggs Benedict to a weekend quiche. Specials are only served 7:00 a.m. to 10:00 a.m. but are extraordinarily well priced. On our visit, the daily breakfast specials were less than $5. The atmosphere alone (whether sitting inside or outside) is worth $5. Other tantalizing menu items include the wild mushroom and asparagus omelet, a calabacitas omelet, and the almond-lemon French toast. We enjoyed the daily special breakfast quesadillas that came with nice crispy bacon and had sour cream drizzled on top with a side dish of salsa. The old fashioned oatmeal was delicious and a nice light breakfast option. We ordered a scone for our sweet tooth, and it was moist and sweeter than many scones we have had. A delicious breakfast dessert.

If, for some reason, breakfast at the St. Francis isn't your cup of tea— come back in the afternoon for a full cup of hot steaming tea. The St. Francis serves afternoon tea in the hotel lobby daily from 3:00 p.m. to 5:30 p.m.

Recommended reading: The St. Francis, formerly the De Vargas Hotel, benefited from tourism traffic sent to Santa Fe via the Atchison, Topeka, and Santa Fe Railroad. Discover more about the railroad's influence on Santa Fe's tourism by reading Victoria E. Dye's All Aboard for Santa Fe: Railway Promotion of the Southwest, 1890s to 1930s.

Tecolote Café

1203 Cerrillos Road
(505) 988-1362

www.tecolotecafe.com

Breakfast hours:
Daily 7am-2pm
Kid Component: ***
Parking: Plentiful
Area: Cerrillos
Prices: $$

Who, who, who would pass up the Tecolote Café? People driving too fast and aggressively down Santa Fe's Cerrillos Road pass the Tecolote Café every day, that's who! Quite a shame. Breakfast at the Tecolote has high praise from visitors and locals alike. Some of our recent out of town visitors proclaimed, "These are the best blueberry pancakes I have ever eaten!"

The word tecolote is Spanish for owl, and the restaurant is decked out in owl paintings, statues, and wall décor. The menu reports that the restaurant is actually named for a town called Tecolote, about 55 miles northeast of Santa Fe.

The Tecolote's motto is "Great Breakfast—No Toast." You won't miss the toast. Every egg entrée comes with your choice of tortilla or bakery basket. We highly recommend the bakery basket. The basket of muffins will come to the table well before your breakfast arrives. Dive into the variety of muffins, and drown each one with strawberry preserves. You can't be disappointed! Small blueberry and corn bread muffins will begin to fill you up just as your gigantic entrée arrives piping hot from the kitchen.

The Tecolote's breakfast menu is large and specials are offered daily. Be sure to look at the breakfast specials on the board in the main entry hall before you enter the restaurant. Egg dishes and sweet dishes are equally excellent. The breakfast burrito is one of the biggest you will find in Santa Fe. It comes with eggs and your choice of meat, topped with hot red or green chile, and cheese. Egg dishes are served with your choice of beans, potatoes, or posole. All three are good.

The potatoes are thinly sliced, round sections of potatoes, salty and greasy. If you are thinking about your health, there are two great low cholesterol alternatives. The doctor bell is an EggBeaters® dish served with Morningstar Farms® breakfast meats. A healthy version of the breakfast burrito is el corazón contento (made with EggBeaters®, mushrooms, Morningstar Farms® sausages, and topped with chile and light cheese upon request). You can have this heart pleaser with beans or the greasy salty potatoes that are really hard to resist.

The Tecolote also has seven types of omelets with the option to build your own omelet using totally fresh ingredients.

If eggs aren't your thing, dive right into the "Batter Up!" section of the menu. The hotcakes come with the option of ordering one, two, or three pancakes. If you come with a healthy appetite, keep in mind that the hotcakes are as large as the plate and wonderfully thick. Eating the Melba stack is like having dessert for breakfast. It consists of pancakes topped with peaches in a raspberry sauce.

The Tecolote feels like a busy coffee shop on weekdays. On weekends bring your patience and plan for a bit of a wait. In cold weather, you may find yourself waiting in the entry hall in close quarters with other eager diners. In warmer weather, the waiting crowd may spill onto the outside benches. There is always coffee for those waiting. If you are dining alone, or if you don't mind the company of others, there is a community table in the middle room of the restaurant.

Recommended reading: The Tecolote was named after a town in New Mexico. For more information on the history of towns in New Mexico, look into The Place Names of New Mexico *by Robert Julyan.*

Tía Sophia's

210 West San Francisco
(505) 983-9880

Breakfast Hours:
Monday-Saturday 7am-11am
Kid Component: **
Parking: Street and municipal lots
Area: Plaza
Prices: $$

Tía Sophia's may have one of the best-kept secrets in town as it serves up some of the most authentic New Mexican food all around. The restaurant's founder, Sophia Aleck, is not a native New Mexican, but emigrated from Greece in the 1930s. Another one of Tía Sophia's greatest secrets is that it has the best booth seating in the state of New Mexico. Tall high-backed wooden booths cloak breakfast diners in private boxes that line the walls of the restaurant. There are eleven booths that seat two people, five booths that seat four people, and a big booth to seat five or more people. The booths allow for the ultimate private conversation and the quiet enjoyment of the great entrées served at this long-time Santa Fe favorite.

There are also café tables at Tía Sophia's, and some of the tables near the windows in front of the restaurant allow for fun tourist watching as people wend their way down San Francisco Street. The reality of eating at Tía Sophia's, however, is that you can't be too picky about where you are sitting—just be glad you got inside the door and get to try this magnificent food. Even on weekdays there is likely to be a short wait for a table, but all waiting is well worth your time.

If you find yourself waiting for a table, look across the street at Santa Fe's historic Lensic Theater where Rita Hayworth, Roy Rogers, and Judy Garland performed in the theater's early years. You might also venture down San Francisco Street to one of Santa Fe's independent booksellers, Collected Works, a store that specializes in New Mexico history and architecture, Native American art, New Mexico guidebooks, and New Mexican cooking.

The walls at Tía's are decorated with glittery sombreros, big baskets, woolen Mexican rugs, and fancy old-fashioned Fiesta dresses adorned with row upon row of fancy braid and rickrack. If measured, the rickrack on these skirts would probably reach all the way to Tesuque!

Tía Sophia's menu warns all breakfasters, "not responsible for too hot chile." The chile is hot, but good! The menu is filled with great breakfast selections plus daily specials, which might include: two eggs on a flour tortilla; a quesadilla with eggs, bacon, and cheese; and a breakfast burrito with chorizo, cheese, potatoes, and chile. Other regular breakfast items include a breakfast burrito with your choice of meat, an omelet made your way, eggs and toast with an option for red or green chile and/or salsa, or cereal. We highly recommend visiting Tía Sophia's on Friday and ordering the Friday Special, eggs your way with a blue corn rolled enchilada served with beans, toast, and jam. Enchiladas for breakfast are fabulous! We also adored Tía's posole. It brought tears to our eyes, tasting just like grandpa's posole.

Recommended reading: For a clever twist on childhood favorite The Little Red Hen, *look for* The Little Brown Roadrunner *by Leon Wender. The title character grows corn instead of wheat, ending up with tortillas! And she does it all herself, since pals Jackrabbit, Coyote, and Horny Toad won't help.*

Tortilla Flats

3139 Cerrillos Rd
(505) 471-8685

www.tortillaflatsofsantafe.com

Breakfast Hours:
Daily 7am-5pm
Kid Component: ***
Parking: Plentiful
Area: Cerrillos
Prices: $$

Are you a person who pays attention to things like the Surgeon General's warning on cigarette packages, and "possible side effects" on medicine bottles? Then be sure and heed the warning on Tortilla Flats' menu: "We are not responsible if the Chile is too hot!"

It's not necessary to get up with el gallo rojo to enjoy the New Mexican cuisine here. Breakfast is served until 5:00 p.m. Be sure to remember what you order, because if the word "smothered" is in the description, you may not recognize your tamale, burrito, or huevos rancheros under all that (red or green) chile. Don't hesitate to request your chile on the side.

The "Tortilla Flats Breakfast Special" consists of hash browns topped with two eggs, ham, sausage, or bacon with a blend of white cheddar and jack cheese on a folded tortilla, smothered with red or green chile. It's a good choice for a first-timer. Several breakfast dishes are served with salsa on the side, and the salsa is fabulous. If you are experimental, you may want to ask for salsa on the side with any of the egg dishes.

A friend of ours swears by "El Tamale," which comes with two eggs any style, smothered (there's that word again!) with red or green chile and beans, served with corn or flour tortillas. (And yes, there's a tamale too!) The "create your own omelet" options and an extensive a la carte section allow the diner almost infinite variety. The "Our Own Recipes" traditional pancakes with blueberries were delicious. Six inches in diameter, with a blueberry in every bite, they were accompanied by hot syrup.

Tortilla Flats is a local favorite and tends to be busy, but you will rarely have to wait for a table. Extra parking is available in the nearby bowling alley lot. You'll see lots of folks reading the *Santa Fe New Mexican* ("The West's Oldest Newspaper, Serving Santa Fe and Northern New Mexico since 1849"), which they may have purchased from one of many vendors who sell papers on the fly at busy intersections around town. The paper is also available from a machine outside the restaurant, but the machine often sells out early in the day.

Both tables and booths are available in three separate dining areas. Families dining with children will find plenty of room for high chairs and a nice breakfast menu for kids. If you're seated in a booth near the window that looks out on the parking lot and are facing Cerrillos Road, you'll have a great view of the Sangre de Cristo mountains (and the Goodwill store across Cerrillos and one block north). The décor is generic New Mexican, with genuine ristras reminding you where the "red" in the official state question comes from.

Recommended reading: In this bilingual collection of folktales by one of America's premier storytellers (and Santa Fe resident) Joe Hayes, nobody could have predicted the weather The Day it Snowed Tortillas/El día que nevaron tortillas.

Zélé Coffee & Café

201 Galisteo Street
(505) 982-7835

Breakfast Hours:
Daily 7:30am-noon
Kid Component: *
Parking: Street and municipal lots
Area: Plaza
Prices: $

If for some reason you're feeling gloomy, you'll be whistling Zip-a-dee-doo-dah and facing a wonderful day if you zip into Zélé for breakfast. Bring your laptop and zap into the Internet in this wireless zone.

One of two Zélé Cafes (the original store is in Aspen, Colorado), this little place with the penguin on its sign is on the busy downtown corner of Water and Galisteo Streets. It looks deceptively small from the outside, but there's plenty of indoor seating at window benches and small tables, augmented by a room at the top of the stairs. If the altitude doesn't bother you, trek to the upper deck. Once there, you can even upgrade to a nifty table for two in a raised alcove by the window overlooking Galisteo Street.

As we know from a wildly popular recent feature film, penguins take zealous care of their eggs. And the staff at Zélé takes zealous care of their omelets, offering a great variety. You could eat here seven days in a row without an omelet repeat. Even the names of the omelets are fascinating: "Eat Your Veggies" (mushrooms, scallions, tomatoes, spinach, and yellow squash); "Green Thumb Frittata" (tomatoes, zucchini, portobellos, onions, spinach); "Palermo Pesto" (grilled chicken, homemade pesto, toasted red peppers, and provolone); "Tremezzo" (prosciutto ham, mozzarella, tomatoes, and basil); "Bayou Bound" (andouille sausage, green peppers, onions, and pepper jack); "Zeus" (kalamata olives, feta cheese, artichoke hearts, spinach, and sun-dried tomatoes); and "Zélé" (chicken, tomatoes, spinach, and garlic). All omelets are served with potatoes and toast or pancakes.

You could go a whole month without duplicating a beverage between the espressos, coffees, teas, chocolate, iced blends, juices, and smoothies.

We enjoyed the Z.B.S., Zélé Breakfast Sandwich (ham, egg, and cheese on an English muffin with chipotlé mayo), which had been our second choice after noticing the "Sold Out" sign taped over breakfast burritos on the chalkboard menu. Lesson: get here early for the burritos! Other options include bagel Americano, pancakes, French toast, and granola.

A decorative cross-hatched wood patio cover provides shade for the outdoor seating area. While we were there, we noticed a couple ride up Water Street on their motorcycle not once, but twice. We had observed them earlier a couple blocks away, where they had taken up two adjoining curbside parking spots to accommodate their pickup and the trailer carrying the cycle. It was fascinating to watch them unload the bike, don their leathers, feed the meters, and finally zoom away.

Recommended reading: Find out how to dispel gloom Santa Fe style in Zozobra! The Story of Old Man Gloom *by Santa Fean Jennifer Owings Dewey.*

Zia Diner

326 South Guadalupe
(505) 988-7008

www.ziadiner.com

Breakfast Hours:
Daily 7am-11am
Kid Component: **
Parking: Parking behind the
restaurant off Montezuma Street,
street and municipal lots
Area: Plaza
Prices: $$

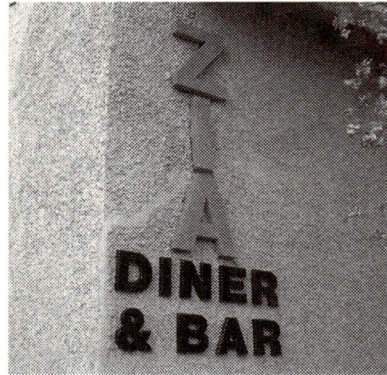

The zia symbol originates from the ancient symbols found at Zia Pueblo in New Mexico. The symbol can be found all over the state, and most prominently on New Mexico's state flag. The symbol represents the sun, the four seasons, four directions, and the four stages of human life. The people of Zia Pueblo also believed that people have four sacred obligations; a person must develop a strong body, clear mind, pure spirit, and a devotion to the community. The Zia Diner may help you prepare for these obligations.

The Zia Diner is located half a mile west of the Plaza. For visitors staying near the Plaza, it is a walk, but plenty of parking should be available during breakfast hours. It is easy to spend a significant amount of time enjoying coffee and breakfast in the relaxed atmosphere of this modern art deco diner with a New Mexico touch. Take note of the thunderbird sconces on the walls and the metal artwork above the bar. Diner walls are hung with local artists' paintings. If you are fortunate enough to sit by a painting you admire, you may be pleasantly surprised to find the artwork is for sale and it is affordable. Comfortable booths and café tables allow for intimate conversation and larger group dining. The Zia Diner has wireless access, so bring your laptop, but don't let it distract you from the amazing food.

Walking in the door of the Zia Diner you will find yourself satisfied. To the right, just inside the entrance sits a case filled with tempting and beautiful pastries, perfect for a breakfast on the go.

Sit-down breakfast options include cereals for the light eater and

asparagus omelets for the more adventurous diners. Zia has New Mexico's traditional breakfast burrito but the menu also includes exciting twists on the New Mexico breakfast palette with migas (tortilla strips with carne adovada, beans, and eggs) and the nutty New Mexican (eggs Benedict with green chile, and corned beef hash on an English muffin).

We can recommend the breakfast burrito if you want a highly traditional New Mexico breakfast without any surprises. Red and green chile is usually mild compared with other restaurants in Santa Fe. Zia uses Taos farm eggs in all of its egg dishes; eggs are from grain fed free roaming chickens. We can also recommend the smoked salmon pizza for those who want to experiment with nontraditional breakfast options. The entrée is a small personal sized pizza that arrives looking handsome on a large dinner plate. Instead of tomato sauce, the pizza crust is coated with cream cheese and topped with thin slices of salmon, capers, and onions.

Recommended reading: Learn more about the zia symbol in famed New Mexico author Rudolfo Anaya's Zia Summer, *the first of four mystery novels featuring private detective Sonny Baca.*

Book List

Title	Author	Restaurant	Page
Alice Nizzy Nazzy, the Witch of Santa Fe	Tony Johnston	Baja Tacos	20
All Aboard for Santa Fe: Railway Promotion of the Southwest, 1890s to 1930s	Victoria E. Dye	St. Francis Hotel – The Club	114
At Ease with the Dead	Walter Satterthwait	Plaza Restaurant	104
Behind the Mountains	Oliver La Farge	Felipe's Tacos	56
Best of From the Plaza, The	William Baxter and Matt Kelly	Santa Fe Baking Company Café	110
Buster Mesquite's Cowboy Band	Tony Hillerman	Horseman's Haven	70
Carlos and the Squash Plant/ Carlos y la planta de calabaza	Jan Romero Stevens	Farmers Market	54
Chaco: A Tale of Ancient Lives	Mark A. Taylor	Inn of the Anasazi – Anasazi Restaurant	76
Chiles for Benito/Chiles para Benito	Ana Baca	Hilton Hotel – Chamisa Courtyard Café	68
Confidence Woman	Judith Van Gieson	Over Easy Café	94
Coyote: A Trickster Tale from the American Southwest	Gerald McDermott	Eldorado Hotel – Eldorado Court	52
Day it Snowed Tortillas/El día que nevaron tortillas, The	Joe Hayes	Tortilla Flats	120
Death Comes for the Archbishop	Willa Cather	Bishop's Lodge – Las Fuentes	22
E is for Enchantment: A New Mexico Alphabet	Helen Foster James	Bagelmania	18
Enjoy Santa Fe More	Jean Cartwright and John Cartwright	Plaza Café South Side	102
Fishing in New Mexico	Ti Piper	Harry's Roadhouse	66
French Women Don't Get Fat: The Secret of Eating For Pleasure	Mireille Guiliano	Café Paris	32
Holding the Reins: A Ride through Cowgirl Life	Marc Talbert	Cowgirl Hall of Fame BBQ & Western Grill	48
Home on the Range: Cowboy Poetry	Paul B. Janeczko	Cottonwoods	44
I Am Here: Two Thousand Years of Southwest Indian Arts and Culture	Andrew Hunter Whiteford	Museum Hill Café	90

Title	Author	Restaurant	Page
Indian Tales from Picurís Pueblo	John P. Harrington	Hotel Santa Fe – Amaya	72
Isabel and the Hungry Coyote/ Isabel y el coyote hambriento	Keith Polette	Meridian Espresso & News	88
Isabel's Daughter	Judith Ryan Hendricks	Cloud Cliff Bakery	42
Jackalope	Janet Stevens and Susan Stevens Crummel	Little Anita's	84
Laughing Boy: A Navajo Love Story	Oliver La Farge	Felipe's Tacos	56
Little Brown Roadrunner, The	Leon Wender	Tía Sophia's	118
Little Gold Star/ Estrellita de oro: A Cinderella Cuento	Joe Hayes	French Pastry Shop & Crêperie – La Fonda Hotel	60
Loretto and the Miraculous Staircase	Alice Bullock	Inn and Spa of Loretto – Baleen	74
Magda's Tortillas/Las tortillas de Magda	Becky Chavarría-Cháirez	Adelita's Mexican Restaurant	12
Making Magic Windows: Creating Papel Picado/Cut-Paper Art	Carmen Lomas Garza	Café Pasqual's	34
Mary Colter: Architect of the Southwest	Arnold Berke	La Fonda Hotel – La Plazuela	78
Miguel Lost & Found in the Palace	Barbara Beasley Murphy	Pancakes on the Plaza	96
My City Different: A Half-Century in Santa Fe	Betty E. Bauer	Café Pink	36
My Dog's Brain	Stephen Huneck	The Burrito Company	28
New Mexico: An Interpretive History	Marc Simmons	Las Salsas	82
New Mexico Ghost Stories	Antonio R. Garcez	La Posada de Santa Fe – El Fuego	80
Only in Santa Fe	Denise Kusel	Pantry Restaurant	98
Other State: New Mexico, USA, The	Richard McCord	New York Deli	92
People I Sleep With	Jill Fineberg	Aztec Café	16
Piñata Maker, The/El piñatero	George Ancona	Bumble Bee's Baja Grill	26
Pink Adobe Cookbook, The	Rosalea Murphy	Café Pink	36
Place Names of New Mexico, The	Robert Julyan	Tecolote Café	116
Pláticas: Conversations with Hispano Writers of New Mexico	Nasario García	Chocolate Maven	40

Title	Author	Restaurant	Page
Red Sky at Morning	Richard Bradford	Plaza Bakery	100
Road to Santa Fe, The	Norman Zollinger	Rio Chama Steakhouse	108
Runaway Tortilla, The	Eric A. Kimmel	Flying Tortilla	58
Sally Goes to the Beach	Stephen Huneck	The Burrito Company	28
Sally Goes to the Mountains	Stephen Huneck	The Burrito Company	28
Santa Fe After Dark: An Illustrated Guide	Bob Eggers	Garduño's Restaurant	62
Santa Fe Hispanic Culture: Preserving Identity in a Tourist Town	Andrew Leo Lovato	Counter Culture Café	46
Santa Fe: A Walk Through Time	Kingsley Hammett	Plaza Restaurant	104
Santos of Spanish New Mexico	Al Chapman	Café Dominic	30
Secrets! of a Los Alamos Kid, 1946-1953	Kristin Embry Litchman	Atomic Grill	14
Serpent Gate	Michael McGarrity	Guadalupe Café	64
Small Adobe House, The	Agnesa Reeve and Robert Reck	Santa Fe Bar & Grill	112
Staircase, The	Ann Rinaldi	Inn and Spa of Loretto – Baleen	74
Tamale Quilt, The	Jane Tenorio-Coscarelli	Posa's El Merendero	106
Taos Pueblo: Painted Stories	Jonathan Warm Day	La Fonda – La Plazuela	78
Too Many Tamales	Gary Soto	El Parasol	50
Tortilla Cat, The	Nancy Willard	Blake's Lotaburger	24
Trail of Painted Ponies, The	New Mexico Public Art Project and HorsePower New Mexico	Los Potrillos	86
Valle Grande: a History of the Baca Location No. 1.	Craig Martin	Adelita's Mexican Restaurant	12
Why I Won't Be Going to Lunch Anymore	Douglas E. Atwill	Celebrations	38
Zia Summer	Rudolfo Anaya	Zia Diner	124
Zozobra! The Story of Old Man Gloom	Jennifer Owings Dewey	Zélé Coffee & Café	122